The Professional's Guide to Successful Management

The eight essentials for running your firm, practice or partnership

Carol A. O'Connor

McGRAW-HILL BOOK COMPANY

London · New York · St Louis · San Francisco · Auckland
Bogotá · Caracas · Lisbon · Madrid · Mexico · Milan
Montreal · New Delhi · Panama · Paris · San Juan · São Paulo
Singapore · Sydney · Tokyo · Toronto

Published by
McGRAW-HILL Book Company Europe
Shoppenhangers Road, Maidenhead, Berkshire SL6 2QL, England
Telephone 0628 23432
Fax 0628 770224

British Library Cataloguing in Publication Data

O'Connor, Carol A.
Professional's Guide to Successful Management: Eight Essentials for Running Your
Firm, Practice or Partnership
I. Title
658

ISBN 0-07-707999-X

Library of Congress Cataloging-in-Publication Data

This data is available from the Library of Congress, Washington DC, USA.

1234   BL   9654

Typeset by Computape (Pickering) Ltd, North Yorkshire
and printed and bound in Great Britain by Biddles Ltd., Guildford, Surrey

This book is dedicated to
Margaret Jane O'Connor.

Contents

Acknowledgements

Much of the inspiration for this book is drawn from experiences with clients and colleagues over the years and I am very grateful for these associations. A more recent influence comes from the nine professionals interviewed for the book's case studies. Their comments considerably enhance the eight management topics which they address. Special thanks to Christine Freshwater, Shane Godbolt, Peter Haigh-Lumby, Richard Klein, Mei Sim Lai, Nina Matheson, Don Pinchbeck, Mike Pleasants, and John Roberts for the generous gifts of their time and attention.

Thanks must also be given to Kate Allen of McGraw-Hill who originally proposed the idea for this book and to Aubrey Wilson who then suggested me as its author. Kate also deserves special mention for editorial patience above and beyond the call of duty and Aubrey for a much-needed introduction to practice development.

I would also like to thank George and Judith Brown for their ongoing influence and interest, and finally say special thanks to my family, Margaret, Marilyn and Jean O'Connor for their astonishing degree of goodwill, support and kindness.

Introduction

PRACTICE ESSENTIALS

Professionals are the 'lone rangers' of working-kind. They place considerable value on their independence and, with society's blessing, they use this autonomy to serve the greater community. Even those who are in partnership or joint practice tend to identify themselves, first, as members of their profession and, second, as partners of their firm. This attitude has a subtle impact on the way that they manage their professional practice. While they acknowledge that they are in business, that business is the provision of advice based upon their individual skills. Theirs is a balancing act where expertise serves business and business, in turn, supports expertise.

This book addresses the unique management needs of professionals and recognizes that many conventional management solutions are actually designed for industry, not the professions. If these solutions are to serve a professional firm, they need to be adapted to match specialized requirements. For example, the conventions of commercial hierarchy break down in circumstances where the senior partner is elected by peers and depends upon their continued support to maintain that position. Leadership and decision making in professional firms provide different challenges than those offered within purely commercial ventures. These differences must be addressed and management suggestions offered so that efforts to improve practice management bring satisfactory results.

Many professionals already have highly developed management skills, gained not only from leading their firms but also through business training. Other professionals choose to delegate practice

1

management because their main interest is in the exercise of their profession rather than the organization of their firm's affairs. Both approaches are appropriate and easily coexist within a firm as long as the strengths and weaknesses of each approach are accepted.

Full and frank discussion among partners about essential management issues leads to agreement about the firm's organization, communication, finance and leadership as well as the development of an innovative approach to information management. When healthy debate reveals that partners do not agree on essential matters regarding the practice, then this discovery allows the creation of new solutions. This book is designed to encourage such debate so that those management areas in need of improvement are thoroughly assessed. Too often, a wish to avoid disagreement leads partners to remain silent about essential business issues. Success depends upon a determined effort to find the best solution while also building healthy peer relationships.

THE AUDIT

The *Management Health Survey* in Chapter 1 is an assessment tool which leads to evaluation of eight management areas of importance to every firm. The Survey questions highlight essential issues from each of these areas and are organized into eight sections, each of which is scored separately. Low section scores indicate healthy practice management; high scores signal a need for improvement. The eight topics are then presented in detail in subsequent chapters. Those sections showing the highest scores provide a good starting point for evaluating a practice. This approach guides the reader to explore, first, those areas which most need attention and, therefore, eliminates the issue of where to begin.

To use an analogy, there is no ideal way to begin untangling a ball of string. It is best to begin work on the most obvious knot and then move on to others in succession as they emerge naturally. This image is relevant to management situations because every area of expertise overlaps each of the others. Exploration of one topic through use of the following survey is likely to bring to light improvement needs in other areas as well.

For example, Chapter 4, Vision and planning can lead to an interest in Chapter 9, Information management, or Chapter 7, Practice development. Because management needs differ from firm to firm, the areas of most crucial importance vary from firm to firm as well. The Contents and Index assist reference to the topics of most relevance to the reader.

THE PROFESSIONAL AUDIENCE

The term 'professional' is generally applied to a variety of activities and roles. There are those who cite licensing requirements as a standard and others who suggest more relaxed and inclusive measures. This book sidesteps this issue by allowing readers to decide for themselves whether the term applies to them and their business. While the case studies, examples and problems describe events from the traditionally accepted professions, they all illustrate issues of interest to the principals of business partnerships in general. Therefore, anyone whose business depends upon the delivery of their own skills, as a service, can benefit from this book. The management ideas and techniques it contains relate to issues prevalent in firms from a broad range of disciplines.

The word 'firm' is used in this book to refer to professional practices, even though it is recognized that their legal status may be partnership, limited company, trust or another form of business. As well, professional firms use a variety of terms to describe their workforce. For brevity's sake, this book uses the term 'partner' or 'practice leader' in reference to those in senior leadership positions. This includes equity and non-equity partners, shareholding members of an incorporated professional firm as well as other senior-level roles. 'Members' on the other hand refers to the whole of the firm's staff: partners, associates, juniors and those in support roles. Finally, those who pay for the firm's services are referred to as 'clients' or, occasionally, 'patients' when medical examples are used.

Examples, problems and case studies illustrate management concepts. Information-gathering forms and analysis questionnaires are also used to encourage readers to assess their firms. The main intention for producing this book is to make current thinking about business management readily accessible to managers of professional firms. Although most professionals are proficient practice leaders, some are not. This book serves its purpose if both extremes find information of interest and suggestions of some value.

1

The practice health check

WHAT IS SUCCESSFUL MANAGEMENT?

Although an entry appears in every standard dictionary for the word, 'success', the diversity of human experience makes a single definition for this term impractical. Individuals bring such personal and idiosyncratic meaning to 'success' that it is equally legitimate to measure it by achievement of goals, accumulation of rewards, feelings of personal satisfaction or some other standard.

The approach presented here emphasizes the exercise of skilful management *for its own sake*. This means that success is an end result, not the actual goal, and that the validity of individual interpretations of 'success' should be recognized. Whether this addresses the need for: achievement of goals, acquisition of rewards or feelings of satisfaction, all of these potentially result when skilful management provides a framework for their pursuit.

> **Success is the creation of a beneficial outcome by applying skilful effort to achieve results.**

This definition emphasizes the role of practice leaders. It is their task to inspire their, often very different, colleagues to act in concert for their clients' benefit and their mutual good. It is essential that these leaders respect different points of view because the members of a practice are more inclined to cooperate when their values and perspectives are respected.

In professional firms, situations exist where:

- partners have varying definitions of success
- firms lack a common view or policy for its achievement
- profession-wide attitudes resist its explicit pursuit.

Practice leaders have the challenge of making explicit these differences in views about success toward developing common goals and enthusiastic collaboration within the firm.

MANAGEMENT SKILL

Although the practice of management is generally discussed as if this were a science, experienced leaders suggest that it is also an art. They admit to using intuition, creative thinking, personal charisma and emotions when managing people and resources. These approaches seem far removed from the rational, logical and impersonal behaviour proposed in management textbooks and business journals. Even so, business management, like art, depends upon having proficiency in basic skill areas in order to produce an excellent performance. The basic skills essential for professional firms are:

- commitment
- leadership
- vision and planning
- decision making
- finance
- development (promotion of services)
- communication
- information management

The *Management Health Survey* which follows is designed to reveal which, if any, of these practice areas need attention. The Survey questions focus on issues essential to the effective management of these areas. The Management Health Survey can be completed separately by individuals or collectively by colleagues who wish to compare their answers. Particularly, where there is strong agreement among a group of professionals about a specific management weakness in their firm, then immediate action should be taken.

Each of the eight sections of the Survey corresponds to a subsequent chapter which addresses each topic in detail. If there is a high score for one area, then reference should be made, first, to the chapter addressing that topic. When reference is made to ideas discussed in other chapters, page numbers are provided to ease review of this supplementary material. There is also a detailed index to allow dipping and browsing for ideas on related topics.

MANAGEMENT HEALTH SURVEY

This survey is designed to assess the overall state of a firm's management health. The issues raised in the following items are not absolute indicators of trouble, rather they are symptoms which need a closer examination. While there are limitless ways for a firm to demonstrate success, there are more finite criteria for a firm *to begin* to show failure.

If one of the items offered below, describes the firm only part of the time, for the purpose of this survey, please accept the item as if it were a fully relevant symptom. Even if a situation or a disruption has been temporary, include it because it *may* provide a 'flag' for a deeper problem.

To offer an analogy, if an individual faints only once or is seized by an unexplained coughing fit very rarely, a doctor takes these symptoms seriously and looks for their root cause. Equally, the manager of a professional practice should take any symptom of trouble seriously until it is fully demonstrated to be superficial and irrelevant. This is a cautious stance and yet it is often proven to be a wise one.

Directions

Please read each of the items. If you believe it applies to your firm, circle the number provided in the score column. At the end of each section, total the numbers which you have circled. These section scores should also be entered at the end of the Survey in the spaces provided so that a total survey score can be determined.

The items are weighted to receive either one or two points. A one-point item is given less weight because it could well be the result of idiosyncracies within a firm. A two-point item refers to an important management issue.

Survey items

Commitment

1   Rivalry among the partners leads to minimal sharing of client leads. 2

2   Clients cannot anticipate who will deal with their affairs or meet their service needs from one contact with the firm to the next. 2

3   There are no obvious contenders for future leadership of the firm. 2

4   The partners responsible for leadership of the practice are frequently too busy with administrative duties to consider strategic growth issues for the firm. 2

5   At least one client during the last year has commented on the firm's inconsistent service or mixed quality of work. 2

6   While the firm's members adhere to the ethical code of their professional body, the firm has yet to publish standards of behaviour or a practice code for its members. 1

7   Each partner's individual success takes priority over the firm's either overtly or covertly. 1

Section total = ___

Leadership

8   Direct attention is not given to staff development or
    retention; at either professional or support levels.   2

9   A sudden resignation of a valued staff member occurs
    at least once each year.   2

10 At least one partner avoids delegating work to associates
    and junior professionals.   2

11 Business meetings are poorly attended, lack direction
    and rarely lead to conclusions or decisions.   2

12 The firm has an autocratic leader who dominates
    discussion and refuses to take advice.   2

13 Principals are unaware of the current concerns of lower-
    level staff regarding health and safety, job satisfaction,
    remuneration, and fair treatment.   1

14 The average age of partners increases by one each year.   1

15 Agreements among partners or by partners with the
    firm's junior members are not kept.   1

16 The assignment of tasks is random or based on staff
    availability, rather than skill levels or experience.   1

                                        Section total =   __

Vision and planning

17 Attempts to set a common direction for the firm end in rows or refusals to discuss specific issues.   2

18 Action is taken as isolated and separate issues arise without reference to long-term objectives or strategy.   2

19 Strategy and plans are developed and yet frequently are not followed or referred to again.   2

20 The firm lacks a three- to five-year financial target which is understood by all the partners.   2

21 Each division within the firm sets its own objectives without checking these with other divisions.   2

22 Partners do not disclose their professional ambitions to each other.   1

23 Partners assume that they agree about the firm's future although they do not discuss this.   1

Section total =   ___

Decision making

24   The firm lacks a legally binding document defining professional and financial relationships.   2

25   Decisions of importance to the firm are repeatedly postponed, even after lengthy discussion or research.   2

26   When communication breaks down among principals, there are no agreed procedures for resolution.   2

27   During the last year, at least one solution to a major problem created disruption in other areas of the firm.   2

28   Support staff lack guidelines for prioritizing assignments as partners overrule their colleagues' requests with requests of their own.   2

29   The partners have similar backgrounds, education and training.   1

30   Decisions made by one partner are undermined and changed by another.   1

Section total =   __

Finance

31 The firm lacks a strong financial manager so that financial advice is taken at random as isolated incidents arise.   2

32 Principals spend money without reference to a budget. Expenses are not monitored.   2

33 The majority of partners refuse to set targets for individual income production or to discuss openly their contribution to the firm.   2

34 Partners resist cutting expenses even though operating costs are paid by overdraft and earnings are below expectations.   2

35 The firm's accounts merge all income and expense so that partners do not have ready access to their contributions and costs.   2

36 The majority of partners are ignorant of the firm's overhead costs and quarterly income needs.   1

37 Resentment is expressed among partners about their having differing perquisites, expenses or workload.   1

Section total =   ___

Development

38 Partners find excuses to avoid activities which promote
the firm.   2

39 At least one partner cannot tell potential clients what
distinguishes their firm from others in clear, specific
terms.   2

40 Efforts to acquire new business are random; the practic
has no real development plan.   2

41 Clients are drawn to the firm by a small minority of
partners.   2

42 The partners depend upon guesswork and assumptions
to determine how their firm is perceived by the public.   2

43 The firm lacks a strategy for systematic development of
client leads through networking.   2

44 Areas used for client contact are untidy, shabby or
difficult to keep clean.   1

45 The firm's members hesitate to ask clients if they are
satisfied. Feedback is not sought.   1

Section total =   __

Communication

46 There are members of the practice who avoid or ignore
    each other for extended periods of time.   2

47 At least once per quarter, a principal complains of not
    receiving vital information.   2

48 The firm lacks a system to ensure that clients' telephone calls
    and letters are answered within a specified amount of time. 2

49 The firm is being sued by a client, a supplier, a former
    employee or another professional firm.   2

50 Clients receive different information about the firm (fees,
    services, procedures) depending on the member of the
    practice who answers the phone.   2

51 At least one partner uses letters or memos in order to avoid
    face to face or telephone contact.   1

52 Office organization discourages informal contact among
    professionals.   1

                                        Section total =   ___

Information management

53 When computer equipment breaks down, the firm lacks
    immediate and comprehensive back-up.   2

54 Confidential files are accessible to determined staff with
    basic technical skills.   2

55 Portable computer equipment is accessible to those who
    are not members of the practice.   2

56 Research is laborious and time-consuming for case and
    project preparation.   2

57 At least one partner does not know what the term
    'network' means in connection with computer technology.   1

58 Partners refuse to agree to updating the computer system
    because there were ill-advised purchases made in the
    past.   1

59 The firm's computer technology is under-used because
    the professional members of the practice do not under-
    stand its benefits.   1

60 Files, papers, reports or other of the firm's documents
    are reported lost by those who have used them, or cannot
    be located by those who wish to use them.   1

Section total = ___

Scoring

Please transfer each section score to the column below.

	Your score	*Maximum score*
Commitment	___	12
Leadership	___	14
Vision and planning	___	12
Decision making	___	12
Finance	___	12
Development	___	14
Communication	___	12
Information management	___	12
Total	___	100

The maximum score is 100 points. Where one of the topic areas has heavily contributed to the total score, then this indicates a good starting point for improving the management of the practice. If the points are spread evenly throughout all eight areas, then this indicates a need for general management assessment.

A score between 75 and 100 points indicates an overall need for improvement. Scores between 50 and 75 points can indicate that the firm is experiencing a challenging period or a transitional phase. It can also highlight that specific partners need management skills development. A score between 25 and 50 points indicates a management system that is basically sound and yet has areas in need of updating and review. A score below 25 points indicates a very well-managed firm.

The following eight chapters provide techniques and suggestions designed to enhance management of professional practices by addressing the issues raised in this survey.

SUMMARY

This chapter offers a definition for success. The issue of management as an art is raised and eight basic skill areas are cited which contribute to an excellent management performance. The *Management Health Survey* is presented as a means for identifying which areas within a firm need improvement.

2

Commitment: the good of the firm

THE CHALLENGE OF MANAGEMENT

When young professionals qualify, they gain social recognition and special status. In return, they adhere to a code of practice which guides them to act in the service of their community. Because their livelihood depends upon maintaining membership and acceptance within their profession, success requires their commitment to ethical behaviour. Successful professional practice is inextricably linked to social responsibility and ethically centred activity. Even the most cynical members of the public recognize this.

During the last years of this century, the average size of professional firms has grown and partnerships, increasingly, have been formed among virtual strangers. This, along with the tendency to merge firms, raises the likelihood that partners accept liability for colleagues' activity without a full awareness of their professional limitations or the extent of their expertise. A balance sheet showing a firm's profitable activity provides little information about the professionals who generated that profit and still less about how they did it.

When partners form a professional firm, they assume joint responsibility for their colleagues' professional and business undertakings. This relationship is legally and financially binding, so joint liability is an important concern. Therefore, issues of ethics, liability, quality of service and reputation are as vital as financial management, decision making and up-to-date electronic equipment when considering needs and 'the good' of a professional firm. Ultimately, if one partner overlooks an ethical concern for even the best of reasons, the entire firm suffers. A need for commitment to the common good of the partners is essential regardless of their number or the rationale for their forming the partnership.

In an industrial situation, when dishonest or incompetent senior managers are discovered, shareholders and the public are generally satisfied by a highly publicized sacking. Fellow managers and directors, if innocent, are usually unharmed. As well, limited liability means that proceedings for fraud or other litigation are generally directed at the actual culprits. In a professional partnership, all of the partners face joint responsibility for their colleagues' errors. A public sacking is as detrimental to a professional firm as it is salutary to a public company. Also, partners share equally the liability for each others' behaviour.

Therefore, the leaders of professional firms must provide exceptional management if they are to address both the complexity of professional ethics and also the crucial issues of business management. Although this is an extremely challenging task, generations of professionals have readily achieved it. It only becomes more difficult now because society's composition and its essential needs are changing. In turn, this means that professionals must reconsider how best to contribute to this change and to adapt their behaviour to serve their clients' newly emerging needs. For example, new issues of confidentiality develop as databases collect seemingly harmless items of information about clients and the activities of the firm's competition. Further, electronic mail and document access create a debate about copyright and ownership of written material. As well, growing awareness of environmental issues requires new thinking about the use of shared physical resources.

All of these issues, and many, many more, mean that definitions of ethical behaviour and community responsibility need to be revised or at least given renewed consideration. Professionals are well placed to provide decisive leadership because they are society's traditional advisers. As the professions evaluate their codes of practice in order to address changing social requirements, firms and individuals must also assess how to serve their clients confidently and with an awareness of this responsibility.

For some, this means new procedures for the management of their practice; for everyone it means avoidance of unnecessary complexity. Simple, streamlined and efficient procedures are far superior to complex, Byzantine and arbitrary ones. The challenge, though, is to balance a wish for simplicity with an awareness of complex business requirements. This situation is more easily resolved when two kinds of management activity are distinguished and then assessed separately. These two refer to the firm's short-term administration needs and its long-term leadership requirements.

The first of these addresses the firm's routine business, its organization and its ongoing maintenance. The second involves decision making for the firm's growth, direction and the quality of service it offers its clients. If too much attention is given to one of these management areas to the exclusion of the other, then this undermines the firm's overall effectiveness. Those practice leaders who are able to coordinate both the short- and long-term needs of their practice, simultaneously create stability and act wisely for the good of the firm.

SHORT-TERM ADMINISTRATION

Specialist divisions

Specialization is one way for a practice to develop a niche within the profession. When this approach is successful, the firm's professionals become the recognized technical experts for a single service area. The benefits of specialization are obvious: concentrated effort and efficient service, client confidence and ease of service promotion, among many others. Also, when a firm develops a niche, then the partners are more likely to act in concert to serve that single client need.

Although there are many firms across the professions which adopt a single-service approach, many others prefer instead to meet a variety of client needs. Within even a small accounting practice, a client can expect to find tax, audit and commercial expertise, as well as other professional services. In larger firms, several specialist areas form separate divisions, departments or sections. Ideally, there is consistent and clear communication throughout these firms and partners routinely refer work across technical boundaries to their colleagues. Specialist areas in the ideal firm increase the services offered to clients and offer improved efficiency, productivity and quality.

Unfortunately, in real life, specialization often creates a barrier to cooperation and justifies the presence of rivalry among the partners. Even when members of a practice verbally agree to act as a team, their need for personal territory and specialist identity is consistently stronger than the attraction of a team-based effort. If technical divisions do lead to individual rather than collaborative effort, then the partners must correct this imbalance.

In general, appeals for cooperation are more likely to succeed when *issues of essential interest* to a given audience are addressed, and the *value of the improvement* is self-evident. For professionals, three issues consistently gain their attention. These are:

- improving the quality of client service
- enhancing the professional standing of the firm
- increasing financial reward.

Even self-absorbed or personally ambitious professionals work harder for the good of the firm when they are reminded that team effort actually benefits those areas which they personally consider to be vital. When a suggestion, request or even demand is presented in *specific terms* which describe its *potential improvement* to the firm's professional standing, the quality of its client service or its income, professionals are better prepared to listen.

This is illustrated by the example of a managing partner who proposes the development of protocols or written procedures for routine tasks. These goals would aim to improve practice efficiency and enhance supervision of juniors and associates. Because the proposal's value is so self-evident, this leader assumes that there will be immediate agreement. It comes as a surprise when the partners later resist the idea, explaining that they are far too busy with fee-generating client work to take on further administration. In response, the determined managing partner proposes that a non-professional administrator write the protocols. When the partners protest that such procedures can only be produced by experts, the managing partner again requests that the partners assume this task themselves. When they refuse a second time, the proposal is put to one side.

Alternatively, the managing partner could present this idea so that it highlights a potential income increase from improved efficiency as well as enhanced client service through quality control. Rather than assume that there will be agreement, this leader convinces the partners to see its merits. Any subsequent discussion should focus on how *specifically* the idea benefits primary professional concerns.

Wheels within wheels

Where there is rivalry among partners or competition across divisions, it is often a serious challenge to create united action within the firm. Although individual partners gain private satisfaction from competition, this does not serve the good of the firm or generate any improvements for the firm as a whole. Rather, it isolates partners and sabotages the firm's ability to function as a single unit. When partners in a spirit of rivalry, for example, withhold client leads from their colleagues, this affects the income generation of the whole firm.

A lack of cooperation can develop unintentionally as well as from conscious design. In a busy practice, the intense pace of work life causes professionals to focus exclusively on their own priorities. Although they are aware of their colleagues' needs, critical deadlines require that they address only immediate goals. This is a lost opportunity for cooperation rather than an avoidance of it. In these cases, specialist divisions and partners' expertise actually encourage a 'sole trader' approach to professional practice.

The challenge is to encourage individual excellence and also avoid fragmented activity within the practice. If the firm is seen by its members to be merely a vehicle for pursuit of individual career interests, then its partners are unlikely to act for the good of the firm or with commitment to their joint responsibilities. The management of such a firm potentially requires extreme vigilance and yet there is an antidote. This emerges from management which reminds the members of the practice of their mutual interdependence, encourages communication and creates standards of professional behaviour for all members to follow. Professionals and partners do not have to like each other, but they can acknowledge that their activities have a continual impact on every practice member.

Coordination needs

The need to coordinate work flow and case assignments provides a moving target for practice leaders. As clients' requirements change and members assume new tasks and responsibilities, their need for support changes. To avoid inefficiency, duplicated effort and outdated policies, the procedures used to run a practice need to be assessed regularly. Because fee generation seems to be the greater priority, partners frequently do not give attention to an administration activity such as this. Ironically, the improved efficiency resulting from examining procedures increases the time partners have available for client work and also lowers the cost of running the firm.

Of course, there are a few firms which seem to thrive with very little management and virtually non-existent coordination. Their apparent success casts doubt on the need for administration, and yet it is the talent and brilliance of the partners within such firms which assure viability. Unfortunately, these firms flourish only when their charismatic leaders are present, active and at the height of their powers. Difficulties arise when they begin to falter or when the loyalty of exasperated staff finally runs out, as it inevitably does.

Badly run firms create the most heartache and headache for those who support the firm's activities in clerical or management roles. In most cases, they work for professionals who do not value administrative skills. Those who lack management ability most, reward proficient administration least so that business support staff receive little appreciation for their efforts.

The eventual defection of staff from the charismatic and chronically disorganized leads to inconsistent and unreliable client service. This, in turn, affects client satisfaction and eventually practice income. However impressive its leaders, a firm cannot remain prosperous for long without effective management and the presence of skilled support staff. Ignoring the administrative needs of the firm is a self-defeating exercise.

Analysis 1

These analysis questions lead to the development of a matrix which indicates the extent of support and cooperation among senior practice members.

1   Across the top of a sheet of paper, note each specialist area offered by the practice.

2   Down the side of the page, list the names of all the firm's partners, leading associates and managers.

3   This forms a matrix. For example:

	Division A	*Division B*	*Division C*
Partner 1			
Partner 2			
Associate 1			
Associate 2			
Manager 1			

4   Next to each person's name, place a mark under the column of his or her specialism.

5   Ask whether this person supports other specialist areas either *formally* or *informally*? If so, place a mark in the appropriate column (this includes client referrals, advice or acceptance of cases and projects).

6   *Agenda* If the matrix is dominated by single marks next to individual names, this is evidence that greater cooperation can be encouraged

among practice members. Alternatively, it could also indicate a lack of information about the frequency or extent of cooperation. In either case, partners should take action: first, to discover how much colleagues cooperate and, second, to encourage its increased occurrence.

LONG-TERM LEADERSHIP

Management of short-term business matters is essential, and it is equally important to develop a long-term management perspective as well. This requires mentally stepping back from everyday business affairs and considering the firm's long-term growth and its quality of service.

Growth

When presented with a growth opportunity, partners occasionally need both discipline and courage to say 'no' to those schemes which look beneficial but do not serve the firm's current interests. These include ill-timed mergers, capital purchases when cash is tight or the acceptance of high-risk business when a portfolio is already risk-laden. Like bargains, opportunities offer value only when they are timely, *genuinely desirable* or advantageous. Of course, the difficulty is to distinguish good opportunities from ill-advised ventures before the choices are made.

The firm which lacks a system for evaluating growth opportunities easily invests time, energy and money in mistaken ventures. This kind of firm grows by following a line of least resistance, by random chance or by changing circumstances. Even if the partners manage routine business with extreme efficiency, they are not managing its growth. This unavoidably leads to underperformance. Decisions about the firm's future are better made through conscious choice rather than by default.

Four practice profiles

This section presents four profiles of professional firms. The examples described in 'Cottage Industry', 'Family Business', 'Overnight Success',

1335032439 8

and 'Corporate Partners' are based on observations of many professional firms. They offer extreme examples of practices which lack plans for growth. The leaders involved do not take a long-term view or consider their overall business needs. Although each of these firms differs in structure, size and personnel, their partners all need to assume greater responsibility for managing practice growth. These examples risk caricature, but specific features of the described behaviour are actually found in many firms.

The cottage industry

This firm begins with as few as one professional and as many as three. Acceptance of new business is limited by the amount of time the partners currently have available. Long-term service contracts, short-term projects and individual cases provide variety and changeable work patterns. The partners avoid prioritizing work and they each are equally prepared to meet client needs as they arise so that a partner specializing in one area readily accepts assignments requiring different skills.

This is a client-centred practice. No matter what they ask, the partners put clients' requests first as each is made. This service approach leads to considerable growth. As client work continues to increase, the partners decide to add new members to the firm. These new people are selected so that they easily fit into the firm and readily adapt to its service orientation.

Managing the practice remains the founding members' responsibility. Occasionally, they complain among themselves that the junior members should take more initiative, be more charismatic and generally show that they have what it takes to lead a firm. Unfortunately, these juniors consistently fall short of the founders' expectations. They are neither initiators nor charismatic leaders. Although they produce work of a high standard, the partners do not fully trust them to manage the most vital aspects of practice business.

Like a wheel with a hub and spokes, the firm continues to turn over with the partners at the centre and their juniors deferring major decisions and leadership to them. There is little sense of collaboration among the more junior members, rather they seek closer ties with the founders and achieve personal success by collaborating with them. As this firm increases in size, management remains vested in its original members. Even when younger members achieve partnership, they never fully gain status as leaders of the firm.

The family business

This firm is founded by professionals who are members of the same family or occasionally by very close friends. Support staff positions are filled by non-professional family members, and generally decisions about the firm are based on input from every family member engaged in the business. Seniority in the firm is determined by seniority in the family with some extra weight given to professional expertise, but not a great deal.

Clients are primarily local and are drawn by word of mouth, friendship and an exchange of favours. The firm creates a sense of 'insiders' and 'outsiders', and their clients enjoy being on the inside. The firm grows steadily and its members are justifiably proud of their achievement. Decision making can be a lengthy process, though, as concerns and input from the whole family are taken into account. At times, client work, projects and other business matters are disrupted because of family issues. Clients understand and accept this because they know that the firm provides a service that is personal and fully attentive to their individual needs.

Unfortunately, there are members of the firm who obviously do not do their share, but this issue is a taboo subject. Family loyalty requires mutual acceptance and understanding and so certain topics are not openly discussed. Instead, less active members are tolerated by those who are more hard-working, talented or conscientious, and yet there is no outlet for anyone to express frustration with this situation.

Occasionally, the firm's senior members discuss who will assume leadership when they retire or whether they should hire 'outsiders' to help with the workload. These discussions never reach a conclusion because the issues seem potentially destructive to the harmony of the firm. In principle, family members readily collaborate with each other on professional matters. In fact, personal antipathy and family jealousy often interfere with full cooperation. When friction does develop, there is little the firm's leaders can do except threaten, cajole or encourage change.

The overnight success

This firm is overwhelmed by its own success. It begins with just a few partners carrying an extensive list of client requirements and later expands when these professionals finally decide to lighten their workload. Because time is so limited, they hire new members in a great rush and then hand them assignments with almost no background explanation. Although they recognize the risk in terms of quality control, they want to seize every business opportunity that comes their way. Time simply does not allow them 'to guide people by the hand' as one partner responded to a newly hired professional's request for more information.

If asked, these dynamic and busy partners would describe themselves as *rocketing* into a bright and eventful future. Each new client is a victory for the firm and the source of the firm's success is never questioned or assessed. Work allocation and management are secondary issues, and the partners genuinely believe that administration of the firm is tangential to its success.

In fact, there are few, if any, business meetings and decisions among partners are often made over the phone. Some of these decisions are not recorded and so other firm members do not know about them. On one occasion, a lease is signed for new premises and one partner only learns about it on the day they move offices. As well, the partners resent paperwork. This approach is copied by newly hired professionals. As a result, support staff are difficult to retain. Those who do stay with the firm often receive contradictory requests and spend considerable time 'fire fighting' and correcting errors.

After approximately three years of high activity, growth reaches a peak. The firm has numerous professional and support staff, a slightly declining workload and a weak organization to coordinate the firm's overall effort. At this point, the firm's partners learn that their profit share has actually decreased from that accrued during their first year of intense growth. They do not know how this could happen. Worse still, they do not know how to discover the source of the apparent difficulty. Privately, at least one partner decides that the fault lies with the others and resolves to leave the firm at the earliest opportunity.

Corporate partners

This 35-partner firm has remained the same size and included essentially the same personnel for many years. Some of the partners, though, believe that they are stagnating and push their colleagues for change. Eventually, although reluctantly, the partners decide to merge with a similar-sized firm. The newly formed practice has 63 partners, and when the partnership papers are signed, everyone seems very pleased by the new arrangement. It is during the following weeks that difficulties emerge over decision making.

Although both firms would have described their management style as participative, one of the original firms delegated decision making to a team of five and the other gathered all of the partners together for frequent and short decision-making meetings. Both groups now realize that they must adopt new procedures because the current size of the firm requires a change from the two previously used systems. The partners decide to organize the firm along corporate lines. Instead of a managing partner and partner-led divisions, they elect a managing director with directors to head each specialist area. These leaders form a board of directors who act on behalf of the rest of the partners.

For those who assume leadership roles within the practice, this new structure is immensely satisfying. Unfortunately, for the others it creates a feeling of being disenfranchised. Although they are partners, they no longer have any direct input into the firm's decisions. They cannot get used to the idea that the firm is now run by a board which does not include themselves.

Management issues

If features from any of these profiles are present in a practice, then it can sensibly be asked: is growth planned or does it occur naturally?

The latter approach is actually management by default and often creates very painful results. In the case of 'Corporate Partners', practice leaders seemingly plan growth but do not consider fully how their choices impact their lives. In 'Overnight Success', the partners create a money-eating practice structure without any controls. The 'Family Business' is also heading for trouble because upon the original partners' retirement, there are bound to be conflicts over leadership. The leadership issue is also a challenge for the 'Cottage Industry' because the founders only hire those with a follower's mentality.

Some of these problem features occur in many firms. For example, many professionals prefer client contact to attending planning or decision-making meetings. If they genuinely believe that meetings with partners are not important, then this is a sign that something is amiss. Those who resist this responsibility either assign little value to the firm's long-term management or else the firm as a whole does not deal with these essential issues in a constructive way during these meetings. In either case, the situation needs attention. When partners ignore long-term issues or refuse to delegate such decisions to others, then they inhibit managed growth for the practice.

As well, many firms 'carry' non-productive partners, as described in the 'Family Business'. Where partners are discouraged from airing their views or from seeking alternative solutions, the practice limits the achievement of its full potential. The well-managed firm encourages debate, discussion, and participation among the partners about important practice issues.

Quality of service

Background

Balancing a need for profit with a commitment to quality is a major concern for anyone in business. Even so, successful professional firms have always offered quality service because professionals know that this satisfies their clients and leads to return business. Also, professional supervisory bodies provide a safeguard for ensuring that their members adhere to performance standards. This supervision is itself a form of quality control.

Currently, there is considerable interest among professional firms for the establishment of quality assurance programmes. Some professionals resist these formal quality initiatives because they believe that this is just another fad. Even so, the interest in quality is now so widespread that it indicates a movement for change rather than a passing trend.

For example, a Total Quality Management (TQM) programme promises increased productivity, efficiency, reliability, profits and motivation throughout an entire workforce. To say 'no' to ideas such as these is like refusing a lottery prize. In fact, when a quality initiative is well-considered, planned and has the complete commitment of a firm's leaders, it does bring great benefit to the business.

Difficulties arise only when such programmes are initiated for short-term or 'quick-fix' success. This approach is bound to fail. A superficial commitment to quality can only do the firm more harm than good. When clients are promised excellent service, they are more critical when they do not receive it. As well, image-orientated or cosmetic 'quality' initiatives demoralize staff. Double standards proposed by top management confuse and disorientate staff who no longer know which performance standards they are to follow.

The relevance of quality programmes for Western professional firms becomes apparent when their Japanese origins are explored because much of this interest emerges from an authentic appreciation of Japanese standards of work. Japanese goods are now associated with the highest quality standards world-wide and yet, following the Second World War, Japan was in complete disarray. To rebuild their industry, Western consultants were invited to work with Japanese managers. The country's subsequent business reorganization was based upon modern Western methods of production and facilities development, *but adapted* so that it integrated Japanese *attitudes* toward work. This hybrid approach included the Japanese concept of *Kaizen* or 'continuous improvement'.

Kaizen is deeply embedded in the Japanese culture and religion and leads individuals to look for ways to improve what they do in some way every day. It also includes the belief that everyone shares equally in the responsibility for creating overall improvement. This blend of *Kaizen* with Western methods of organization created a business culture which is committed to quality performance and is also highly capable of delivering it. The following case study explains this more fully and highlights quality improvement applications for professional firms.

CASE STUDY: INNOVERVE LIMITED

This case study offers criteria for the successful implementation of a quality programme. The two professionals commenting here emphasize that Total Quality Management begins at the top of the firm. It requires a leadership style which encourages everyone to take responsibility for improving the practice. They propose that quality initiatives succeed when firm-wide action is based upon an attitude of continuous improvement and shared responsibility for this throughout the firm.

Don Pinchbeck and Michael Pleasants are British consultants who have both worked in high-level management in Japanese, German, Dutch, American and British firms. They recently founded Innoverve Limited, a company dedicated to the introduction of innovative products, processes and systems. To this endeavour, they bring a profound understanding of Total Quality Management and direct experience of the Japanese approach to quality improvement. Their insight offers benefit to Western professional firms because they know from experience which features of the Japanese model most enhance Western business.

Don explains, '*Kaizen* is a Japanese word which simply means "improvement" and yet to capture its more precise meaning, it has to be translated "continuous improvement". It is at the root of Total Quality Management which some [Western] business people attempt to adopt by starting quality circles [see page 37 for an explanation of TQM]. They are taking techniques born in a different culture and planting them in a Western one. These ideas cannot flourish, just as techniques, because circumstances are not the same here as they are in Japan.'

The drive for quality begins with individuals taking responsibility. In Japan this is natural. When an error is discovered, a group of colleagues gather immediately to discuss what went wrong. In this way, a quality circle emerges as required because everyone *wants* to participate and improve what they are doing. Don says, 'The Japanese believe very strongly that they are responsible for improving what they do every day. Because the idea of continuous improvement is not a *natural* part of Western culture, 80 per cent of all TQM projects which are started in this country [UK] produce negligible benefit. This is because the culture is not there to support each person taking responsibility for creating continuous improvement.'

In Western firms, many leaders adopt an autocratic style. If their firms make a commitment to TQM, this requires a complete change in management style. Don explains, 'We have many leaders [in Western firms] who act like captains on the bridge barking orders. If you put TQM into a company with autocratic management, it will fail because in this model, only people at the top can offer ideas for improvement. In the firm with a commitment to continuous improvement, people talk freely. They are invited to contribute, learn, ask questions and admit that they do not understand. This creates an atmosphere of shared commitment to the firm and encourages suggestions for improvement from everyone.

'Practice leaders set the tone for increased participation by first recognizing expertise *at all levels* of the firm. When people *know* that their contribution is valued, they feel drawn to offer ideas and suggestions for improving the practice.' The show of respect for ideas freely offered is a quality initiative of far greater benefit to the firm than the adoption of monthly quality circle meetings. Don adds, 'Encouraging ongoing discussion about improvement leads to the creation of an "early warning system" where practice members volunteer information about outside events which could impact the firm'.

Michael suggests that, 'A quality initiative recognizes each person's ability and expertise and so harnesses that person's willingness to improve even a small area of the practice. This improvement *moves up* through the firm.' Don adds to this, 'The person at the top no longer has to be everywhere and know everything because there are constructive ideas and early warnings coming from all parts of the firm.

In Japan, this is the norm and it is the one attitude above all others which creates Japan's competitive advantage.'

Don continues, 'Quality is not about systems and procedures. I have difficulty with BS 5750 for example. Although this [quality standard] documents what people do, it often doesn't take the company forward. If you do something consistently well or consistently badly, BS 5750 will ensure that you continue to do it either consistently well or consistently badly. It is a means of *formalizing* what you do [see page 39 for an explanation of BS 5750].

'To really take on a quality approach, the person at the top of the firm has to make a declaration and give some clear signals which show a new vision for the future. This person must run up a flag for everyone to see which says, "I want your contribution and if you offer this we'll have a successful company and a great time together. Mistakes are for learning, not for punishment." Belief in a new approach won't be spontaneous. The leaders' task is to show everyone that things are changing and at the same time encourage them to pull together.'

To this Michael adds, 'If the person at the top has set a style of openness, contribution and enjoying work together, then quality cascades throughout the company. There is an issue, though, within some organizations. Autocratic leaders have often recruited people who want direction and who may work well in a less participative environment. This kind of firm cannot help but underperform. This is because it depends on one brain seeing into the future and driving the firm forward. In a more open environment, you have everyone working to bring the organization forward and at a very rapid rate.

'Junior members particularly must understand the firm's direction, its vision and objectives and how it operates. This allows them to feel confident when they represent the company. In some firms, this information represents power and so leaders withhold it. It is far better to release information into the organization because then everyone can move the vision forward as a result.' A quality initiative is the joint responsibility of the whole firm, from the least to the most powerful person within the practice.

QUALITY INITIATIVES: TQM and BS 5750

When practice leaders make an explicit commitment to quality service, they initially gain their clients' attention. When these firms actually meet their quality standards, business can only prosper. Word of mouth promotion is always a powerful endorsement, and quality performance encourages this.

When clients select a firm, they look for consistency, continuity of service, efficiency and cost effectiveness, confidentiality, adequate records and back-up, and commitment to the contract for service. Informally, they ask their associates for recommendations and try to discover as much as possible about a firm before making any initial contact. As a substitute for personal referral, adherence to quality standards is a powerful endorsement for the firm and, therefore, provides considerable advantage over the competition.

Don Pinchbeck and Michael Pleasants highlight the many benefits of a quality programme and emphasize its applications for a professional firm. Among the tangible benefits are consistent and reliable service, an inspired and committed workforce, a promotional advantage over the competition, decreased liability, improved productivity and cost-cutting through efficiency. With quality-control procedures in place, performance is monitored so that uniform standards are consistently met. This leads to the resolution of problems before crises arise, and the identification of training needs as a result of supervision.

There are also intangible benefits. A published quality policy not only impresses clients, it also affects staff. People like being associated with a quality-oriented company and they know that the firm's good reputation reflects favourably on themselves. A new level of *esprit de corps* leads to decreased absences and complaints of stress. Another indirect benefit is an enhanced stature for the firm. When problems do arise, clients are more likely to seek resolution with the firm's management rather than complain to the relevant regulatory body. Firms with a quality programme in place are more likely to be assumed innocent until proven guilty.

There are two quality initiatives of particular relevance to professional firms. These are Total Quality Management (TQM) and

British Standard 5750 (BS 5750). The distinctions between them make them applicable to different professional disciplines. Table 2.1 on page 41 summarizes their differences and similarities.

Total quality management

TQM is a far-reaching quality programme which requires everyone within the firm to examine issues of quality performance. It leads, in most cases, to a thorough evaluation of the firm's values and beliefs so that complete change is created in the way the firm conducts its business. The TQM firm is a client-centred and quality-focused practice, with every member taking full responsibility for this. The model for this initiative is frequently presented as a triangle, so that the three essential features of the Total Quality approach are given equal weight. These features are: management commitment, motivated workforce and measurement of quality (see Figure 2.1).

All three issues must be addressed when creating an environment which actively promotes quality. Because each firm is unique, a TQM programme is designed so that it meets a firm's individual needs. The final result, though, must be the same for every firm, that is, a shared culture based on a commitment to quality through continuous improvement.

'Culture' in this context refers to the firm's values, knowledge base and its expertise. To create a common culture, the firm must:

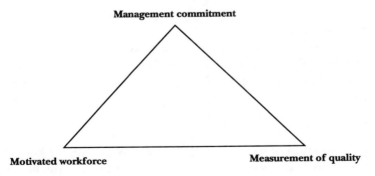

Figure 2.1   Total Quality Management Model.

- establish a common purpose for its activities
- set out procedures which achieve this purpose
- develop a common language
- provide ongoing education and training for skill development.

TQM requires active participation from the firm's top management who must offer structure, resources and enthusiastic support. This programme leads to profound change because those who invest in its success must invest so much time, energy and finance that they clearly lose by not meeting their initial commitment. Also, they find it equally obvious that the potential gain is well worth the challenge. There are four actions which contribute to a successful TQM programme. Each is of equal importance to the achievement of quality awareness.

1   A survey of all firm members should be made to discover the current attitudes and commitment to quality. This not only provides valuable information, but also establishes a baseline against which future attitude change can be measured. The survey items should establish the extent of quality awareness, where this awareness already exists and where quality awareness needs to be developed.

2   The firm's most senior members should make a clear and public statement that quality is a way of life for the firm. They should refer to this commitment to quality in the firm's mission statement and also publicly endorse the basic principles and values of quality performance.

3   Everyone in the firm should become involved in discussions about quality and actively explore how this initiative affects their own work. Where training needs are identified, action should be taken to provide the necessary skills. Education and training are integral parts of a quality programme.

4   Performance should be monitored with a view to creating continuous improvement. TQM is successfully implemented when everyone takes responsibility for monitoring the quality of the firm's work.

Guidelines for achieving TQM are outlined in a British Standards Institution publication, BS 7850. This standard is a British initiative, and International and European Community standards are yet to be developed. The address of the British Standards Institution (BSI) is included in Appendix I.

British Standard 5750

British Standard 5750 (BS 5750) is a quality standard published by British Standards Institution (BSI). It corresponds to International Standard 9000 (ISO 9000) and European Community Standard 29000 (EN 29000). BS 5750 outlines all of the features necessary for a quality assurance programme. Unlike TQM which embraces *all aspects* of quality performance, BS 5750 emphasizes the development, maintenance and improvement of a practical working management system. This system assures quality through the implementation of published and monitored administrative procedures.

Firms obtain a registration certificate from BSI when they successfully pass an audit. This audit is impartial and based on an exhaustive examination of a firm's inner workings. It indicates that all aspects of a company have been examined and that the auditors are fully satisfied that reliable performance standards are in place.

The audit tests whether the firm's procedures as they are presented in the firm's quality assurance manual are followed when work is actually completed. This measures compliance to a system and, therefore, assures the client that the specifications they expect are fully met. 'Quality', in this context, means consistent, reliable, uniform service *which matches* a promised performance standard.

The requirements for BS 5750 are rigorous and emphasize the commitment of top management to quality assurance. Those firms which successfully pass an audit have met the following five criteria

- a published quality policy signed by senior management
- a rigorous examination of all activities to ensure that these reflect a philosophy of quality
- a full assessment of administrative systems

- a designated person to supervise maintenance of quality standards throughout all activities
- a description of these standards and activities in a company manual.

The emphasis of BS 5750 is on administration which assures quality and yet it leaves unchallenged some key issues. These include what actually constitutes quality and a quality performance, and whether the specified procedures lead to the best possible performance. Critics of BS 5750 question its benefits for professional firms because it offers only a partial solution to the development of a quality programme. They also suggest that the necessary paperwork is initially time-consuming and the expense of application, audit and annual fees seems high.

These issues alone should not discourage exploration of BS 5750. For those professions which require technical precision, such as architecture, chartered surveying and engineering, BS 5750 is a valuable part of a quality control programme. In fact, many leading corporations now require subcontractors and suppliers to have BS 5750 certification. However, firms such as law and accounting, BS 5750 is perhaps an inappropriate choice because the audit requires the review of confidential records.

With regard to paperwork, firms actually find that BS 5750 decreases rather than increases their need for unnecessary paperwork because duplicated effort is eliminated and reliable procedures often make paper follow-up unnecessary. The paperwork issue is also addressed by new computer applications. There is software available for BS 5750 so that computerized procedures can easily be updated and approved through electronic mail. The cost of BS 5750 should be considered against the potential benefits of competitive advantage.

Effort made toward achieving TQM considerably eases the process of gaining BS 5750 certification. The emphasis on procedure and administration for BS 5750 also contributes to TQM if the workforce has been encouraged to discuss thoroughly all issues surrounding quality performance. Also, BS 5750 requires a complete commitment to quality assurance and a policy statement from the firm's top management (see Table 2.1 for a comparison of BS 5750 and TQM).

Table 2.1:   BS 5750 and TQM Comparison

	BS 5750	**TQM**
Internationally recognized standard	Yes	Yes
Competitive advantage	Yes	Yes
Requires top management support	Yes	Yes
Widespread employee involvement	Yes	Yes
Exclusive emphasis on administrative procedures	Yes	No
Requires an external audit for certification	Yes	No
Requires a detailed procedures manual	Yes	No
Audit exposes confidential records	Yes	No
Emphasis on continuous improvement	No	Yes
Emphasis on communication	No	Yes
Emphasis on shared values and knowledge	No	Yes
Emphasis on all aspects of quality	No	Yes
Achieved by means of one-off training	No	No
Achieved by poster campaign	No	No

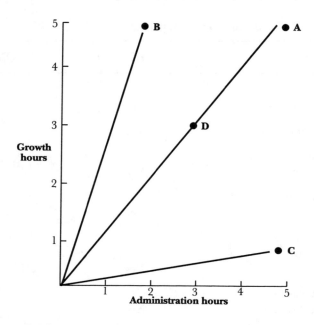

Partners	Administration hours (average per week)	Growth hours (average per week)
A	5	5
B	2	5
C	5	1
D	3	3

Figure 2.2   Balancing short- and long-term needs.

THE BALANCING ACT

The partners' ability to shift perspective from the firm's short-term administration to its long-term leadership needs provides the firm with balanced management. In highly complex firms, the managing and senior partners spend most of their administration time on practice growth and quality control and very little time on operational or routine business matters. This is delegated to others. In smaller firms, partners tend to share equally in the responsibility for both long- and short-term management. Because these two management areas are equally important, practice leaders need to ensure that they give appropriate attention to both areas as required.

Figure 2.2 presents a matrix which plots the time partners A, B, C and D spend on operational management as opposed to growth management. Individual A gives an equal amount of time to both. Individuals B, C and D apportion their management time so that the amounts are unequal.

It is not really possible to suggest an *ideal balance* for these two functions because circumstances vary from firm to firm. Even so, a firm's partners decide what they believe is the correct balance, then monitor and adjust this as necessary. When partners vary from their own estimate of a proper balance, then that is the time to assess their behaviour.

As well, the level of responsibility which a partner assumes within the firm indicates which management perspective should receive greater attention. For example, if individual C from Figure 2.2 is the firm's managing partner, then the other partners should express some concern. The managing partner who uses an average of five hours per week for general administration compared to one hour for managing growth should at least question this balance. It is useful if partners discuss among themselves how they apportion management time as individuals and what they believe is best for the firm as a whole.

Analysis 2

1   Score the effectiveness of your firm's everyday administration of business.

1 ←———————————————————————————→ 5
Poor   Excellent

2   Score the effectiveness of your firm's coordination of growth and quality focus.

1 ←———————————————————————————→ 5
Poor   Excellent

3   Does your firm have a number of obvious contenders for future leadership of the firm ?

Yes   No   Possible

4   Is there an outlet for members of the practice to debate long-term decisions and the firm's policies?

Yes   No   Possible

5   Do all partners recognize the importance of setting priorities which balance routine administration with practice growth and quality.

Yes   No   Possible

6   Using the format of Figure 2.2, how do you apportion manage-ment time? (Refer to time records for this.)

7   What is your estimate of how your colleagues apportion their management time?

8   Using a piece of graph paper produce a matrix charting a point for each partner or professional?

9   Draw lines from zero to each point in order to highlight any differences.

If those with most responsibility for the firm show a low time commitment to growth management and a high commitment to routine administration, then it should be asked: Who is leading the firm? If only one partner gives a high time commitment to growth, then the question is: How wise is this? Creating a perfect balance is not required, but awareness that it is an important issue for practice success is crucial.

PROBLEM – ANALYSIS – DISCUSSION

Problem
Until two years ago, this firm of solicitors grew without a sense of conscious planning on the part of its ten partners. Instead, they

responded to client demand and business circumstances when deciding to add new services or recruit members for the firm. This informal approach worked well for them until recently when the firm merged with a smaller practice offering similar services. The original partners believed this addition would widen their client base and also increase their ability to serve their clients better.

The partners from the two firms brought with them very different styles of working. The larger ten-partner firm emphasized open communication and face-to-face discussion. The four partners in the smaller firm had been dominated by one charismatic leader and left decision making largely to him. Only recently, did partners in the larger firm learn that their new partners had never fully discussed the merger and did not realize what the change would mean to them. This provided an explanation for their new partners' extreme resistance to any form of collaboration with the larger firm. They even refused to merge their specialist divisions with those of the larger firm's although technically the services offered were very similar.

The terms of agreement drawn up at the merger allowed both firms to exercise a degree of independence. The intention was to allow a natural process of integration to occur. In fact, the two firms simply coexisted side by side without an integration of services. As time passed, the partners from the smaller firm deepened their resistance to sharing clients or workload. This was most detrimental to the members of the larger firm, who put considerable time and energy into resolving the merged firm's difficulties. Indirectly, all 14 of the partners have been affected because their income generation has decreased as a result.

Analysis

Please answer the following questions as if you are an outside consultant invited by the managing partner to help integrate the firm's two subunits.

1   What is the first action you would recommend?

2   How should an agenda be prepared for a joint meeting of all 14 partners?

3   Is there a future for this firm as it is presently organized?

4   Would it be appropriate to suggest a demerger?

5   If so, what indicates that this is a good idea?

6   If not, what changes must occur?

Discussion

The first step would be to convene two separate meetings, each to be attended by the partners of the premerger firms. This makes explicit their continued division. Although they *should* be an integrated unit, it does not help to ignore the fact that they are not. During these meetings, the consultant should seek to discover if there is will on both sides to form an integrated practice. Partners from the two groups should propose agenda issues for a later joint meeting of both groups. There certainly does not seem to be a future for the firm as it is presently organized. The partners' behaviour has affected their income generation and there is no reason to believe that this loss will not continue.

During a joint meeting, the agenda items developed during the two preliminary meetings should be addressed. This meeting requires leadership that encourages participation and yet prevents domination by very vocal partners. At this time, the idea of a demerger should be discussed

It certainly looks as if demerger is a likely possibility. Because the smaller firm has resisted any open discussions, considerable bad feeling has developed among their colleagues in the larger firm. Unless they show a radical change in attitude, it is unlikely that the 14 partners can make a fresh start. Given their history of resistant behaviour, a new era of good relationships is difficult to imagine. These issues must be brought into the open if any progress is to be made.

SUMMARY

This chapter emphasizes the need to distinguish between short- and long-term management needs. Short-term issues include encouraging partners to work cooperatively and coordinating effort so that the firm runs efficiently. Long-term issues describe the need to manage and plan for growth as well as to monitor quality. The differences and similarities between BS 5750 and Total Quality Management are explained. Also a method is suggested for partners to determine if they are balancing their management effort overall.

3

Leading leaders

THE LEADERSHIP CHALLENGE

More than anything else a successful firm requires good leadership. Its professionals can be experts in their field, good managers of their specialist area, and yet they also need leadership skills to direct the firm's overall activities in a consistent, coherent and comprehensive manner. This chapter addresses essential leadership needs for professional firms. It emphasizes those practice areas which need most attention, and the skills, qualities and personal insights essential for leaders to fulfil their role.

Currently, there is a tendency for those in positions of power to resist proclaiming themselves 'leaders'. It has become a title used at an annual dinner for praising a colleague's work, or softened by qualifications such as, 'party leader', 'team leader' or 'project leader'. Even the ruthless and ambitious avoid stating publicly that leadership is their aim in life. Although idealistic teachers promote the qualities of leadership in schools, and academics continue to research leadership issues in universities, those who carry leadership responsibility in public are diffident about saying, 'I am the leader.'

This title is certainly held in far less repute than it was at the start of this century, and yet this is not surprising given the gruesome abuses of power seen in world politics. For many people, these abuses are associated with the *function* of leadership rather than the *personalities* of specific leaders. Of course, talented, powerful and astute individuals continue to assume the roles of director, manager, administrator, supervisor as well as managing or senior partner. They simply use greater subtlety when referring to the extent of their power.

If this reticence is merely an issue of language or the result of personal taste or background, then resistance to the term is not a cause for concern. Alternatively, if it stems from a reaction to historic power abuse, an over-emphasis on group responsibility or a belief that groups lead themselves, then it is a crucial matter. Leaders who avoid asserting their legitimate authority with clarity and confidence actually provoke confusion and anxiety among their colleagues. They create a vacuum where there should be a focus of authority.

By refusing to acknowledge their own power they disempower others because their colleagues lose their representative, their guide and their coach. These essential leadership functions are unfilled when 'nice guys' refuse to take full responsibility for their leadership role. Truly nice guys, both men and women, are more honest to themselves and to others. Assuming the mantle of legitimate authority in a responsible manner invites colleagues to debate and challenge that authority in the interests of the firm.

This aversion to the role of leader is currently common practice. Indications of this are shown by partners' remarks which include:

- 'Our meetings lead themselves.'
- 'We don't want or need strong leaders in our firm.'
- 'Our firm avoids old fashioned leadership.'
- 'The managing partner is just a figurehead for the firm, not a leader.'
- 'We don't believe in hierarchy.'

All of these comments are made by sincere professionals who confuse a potential abuse of power with leadership. There is an alternative approach which recognizes that leaders assume both power and responsibility. They cannot have the role without the power. Denial of this means underperformance. This issue needs to be resolved because the role of professional is inseparable from that of leader or from that of manager. In a professional firm, there are as many leaders as there are partners. Even those who believe that their technical skill and case management are paramount are also responsible for setting the firm's goals and guiding its activities. This makes the task of leading fellow leaders even more challenging as each partner's opinion has equal weight and value in any debate about the firm's activities.

Leader and follower paradox

A modern definition of leadership emphasizes the mutual dependence of leaders and followers. Essentially, this acknowledges that without followers there are no leaders. Although their responsibilities are different, the contribution of both roles is crucial to any group effort. The following definition of leadership highlights this idea.

> Leadership is the ability to present a vision so that others *want* to achieve it. This requires skills to build relationships as well as to organize resources.

It suggests that leaders may formulate vision, but their followers must be willing to accept it. Otherwise, the vision is just a meaningless dream.

In professional situations, there are added complications. Even those professionals who are not partners within the firm have a certain status as expert authorities. They gain this through membership of their profession and it affects their expectations of how they should be treated as professionals. As a result, relationships among colleagues are often laden with implicit agreements and unspoken rules. Breaking these carelessly, even inadvertently creates serious problems. Under-estimating the average professional's personal sense of status hinders leadership effectiveness because it causes unnecessary aggravation.

However expert, important and respected practice leaders are, they are also wise to remember that the pinnacle of any hierarchy rests on the bottom step of some other, larger hierarchical grouping. No leader is all-powerful and free from others' influence (see Figure 3.1). The individual who chairs a multinational answers to shareholders. The politician depends upon voters. Even the totalitarian ruler eventually must face the larger international community. Having attained the peak of influence, leaders quickly discover the constraints placed upon them.

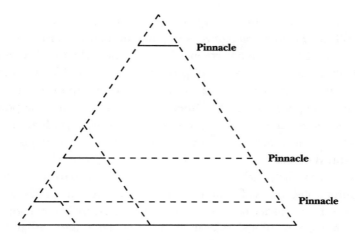

Figure 3.1   The 'top' is relative.

Those who forget this, risk isolating themselves and their firms from new challenge and outside influence. Not only must the leaders of a practice know how to exercise authority, they also need the wisdom and tact to accept others' leadership on occasion and follow. The skills associated with following lack glamour and yet, paradoxically, contribute to the kind of leadership which produces results. These skills include the abilities: to receive advice and guidance, to obey legitimate constraints, to listen carefully to colleagues' ideas, to acknowledge power in others and, when appropriate, to express humility.

Leaders who also possess skills of 'followership' are able to cooperate with the ideas and insights of their colleagues. The direction they offer the firm is, therefore, based upon a united partnership. These leaders are prepared to honour agreements because those which they make are based upon accurate information and shared commitment. As well, such behaviour is inspiring and colleagues want to support this kind of leadership effort.

POWER AND POLITICS

Power is both fluid and fixed at the same time. It is possible for those who possess it to increase or decrease the power they hold without necessarily affecting the ability of their colleagues to hold power as well. Effective leaders recognize the source of their power as well as the limitations of their empowerment. This enhances their ability to assess the potential success or failure of projects, schemes and ideas. For some leaders, this assessment occurs so rapidly and automatically that they refer to it simply as 'instinct'. Others evaluate power and the powerful both consciously and rationally. Whatever method individuals use, they benefit from accurately assessing their own and others' ability to hold and express power.

Sadly, those who lack this skill stand among the arrogant, the rude, the bumptious, the self-deluded, the impractical, the naive and the innocent in that order of self-menace. As leaders, their behaviour is an imposition upon others' tolerance and understanding rather than a contribution to successful business. Ignorance about power, its uses and deployment is an inappropriate quality in any professional. It not only undermines technical effectiveness, but also professional relationships because it leads to serious misjudgement. There are four kinds of power commonly expressed in professional firms. These are:

- designated or legitimate power
- expert power
- charismatic power
- information power.

A choice should be made about the kind of power to express when deciding on appropriate leadership behaviour. For example, professionals assume the responsibility of expert power when they are accepted into their profession. This power is independent of a specific role within a firm and is based upon the professional's training and ability. They are authorities in their own right when they then join a professional practice.

Successful firms depend upon their ability to exert their professional authority wisely and well. When leaders of these firms assign tasks, they exercise legitimate power as managers of their firm. Alternatively, when they use charm or influence to encourage or inspire, they express charismatic power. Skilful leadership requires conscious choice about employment of power.

Designated power

This power is linked to specific roles or positions within the organization. For example, a department manager's power to manage is drawn from the designated position of 'manager'. When this individual leaves that position, the power to manage that department is passed to a replacement. The firm's organizational chart indicates all of the sources of designated power by highlighting the firm's management requirements.

The functions which designated leaders fulfil include: planning, decision-making and controlling resources, information and risk. Their task is to fulfil these functions in a way that inspires their colleagues to want to contribute their best performance. Specific leadership roles should each have a job description so that the extent of an individual's power is made clear.

Associated with designated power is the authority to reward or punish others within the organization. A 'carrot and stick' approach to management is less effective within professional firms. It depends too heavily on power being vested in only a few top positions. Because professional practice includes many 'tops', as partners, they jointly own the carrot and the stick and share responsibility for their use. Also, non-partner professionals hold expert power themselves. In professional firms, reward and punishment should be determined case by case through direct communication with individuals.

Expert power

Whenever professionals draw on their own expertise to advise their clients, they employ expert power. They also express this through writing, lecturing and research. As their standing within their profession grows, their expert power increases. This power exists separately from designated power and has little to do with the firm's official hierarchy. Those who are leaders in technical matters are not necessarily suited to assuming management roles within the firm.

Even so, expert power is undeniable, and the wishes of those who possess it should be considered. When valued technical experts avoid formal leadership roles, they tend gradually to withdraw from decision-making activities within the firm. Occasionally, this leads to their more active colleagues' forgetting the importance of consulting them when important decisions are made.

If their priorities are ignored or a decision angers them, they are, from their viewpoint, justifiably upset at not being consulted. Practice leaders need to maintain strong and informal links with valued experts in the firm. However much these professionals lack interest in practice politics and decisions, they should always be kept fully informed and urged to participate.

Charismatic power

This source of power is linked to personality. It is essentially the ability of one individual to influence another through force of character. Charisma emanates from some people and not from others. In traditional theories of leadership, charisma is emphasized as an essential trait and the foundation of 'natural leadership'. Although modern theorists challenge this idea (see 'The adaptive leader', page 64), the popular press continues to promote the importance of charisma.

It is undoubtedly a valuable trait, and charismatic professionals do benefit their firms considerably. Using charm, style and grace, these leaders draw new business and indirectly promote the practice through all of their contacts. However, this is also the source of power that requires the most careful handling. When a member of a firm has both charisma and expertise, the leaders of the practice have a valuable colleague. Their main challenge is to discourage any prima donna behaviour. When a colleague shows more charisma than expertise, then this professional should assume roles which emphasize human contact and promotion of the practice rather than technical achievements.

Information power

This kind of power is most frequently held by a non-professional practice member. Its source is a person's possession of information which is critical to the functioning of the firm. Wherever there are long-serving clerical staff, there are human memory banks which can retrieve pieces of information, as needed, from either physical or mental files. The sudden loss of one of these power sources can cause an immediate breakdown of communication and even loss of client contact. Although information power is vital for the success of the firm, its value is frequently overlooked by professionals.

All support staff should be encouraged to share information. Their work routines should be documented to avoid over-dependence on specific individuals as sources of information. Alternatively, staff should be treated so that they are encouraged to stay within the firm. Their consistent presence is another form of information power. Long-serving individuals *understand* the firm's priorities and procedures. They often instinctively contribute the right response to unprecedented situations and are valuable allies during times of crisis. This quality of support enables the firm's professionals to perform well because the available information directly contributes to their delivery of expertise.

Information power is also provided through technology and computer links with data resources outside of the firm. This aspect of information power is presented in Chapter 9, Information management.

CASE STUDY: GERALD EVE CHARTERED SURVEYORS

The purpose of this case study is to illustrate the importance of leadership within a professional firm. The Director of Finance and Administration whose remarks are featured here seeks to understand the wishes of the firm's partners through consistent communication and a consultative approach. He then implements these through delegation and careful monitoring of results.

Gerald Eve Chartered Surveyors is a long-established and highly respected professional firm with 35 partners. Its management is delegated to a small management committee one of whose number is Peter Haigh-Lumby, a chartered accountant. He is responsible for the day-to-day control of the firm's finance and its administration needs.

Because Peter acknowledges that there are challenges in leading other leaders, his philosophy is that professional management is an essential for running a professional practice, a view which is generally accepted and appreciated by professional colleagues.

He says, 'Partners in professional firms are qualified in their respective professions. They may have gained experience in managing a firm themselves, but they are unlikely to be professionally trained managers. A firm's management team can be smaller if there is a professional manager as part of that team. This relieves the need to have an inordinate number of partners actively involved in a management role because you can delegate these responsibilities to one trained individual.'

In a partnership, those who own the business also work in the business. They need to be convinced that professional management actually enhances the running of the firm. Peter says, 'For the partners of a firm to have confidence in your ability, you have got to prove yourself over a period of time. This means having a general understanding of the business, in my case chartered surveying; it means also understanding the aspirations of those individuals who make up the firm.' He believes that this understanding is vitally important if management of the practice is to succeed and be effective.

Peter explains further, 'During my first couple of months in this position, I spoke individually and in confidence to each of the owning partners. Even though the recruitment procedure to bring me into the firm gave them extensive information about me and my background, I asked them if they wished to know anything further. Then I asked them two questions: What did they expect me to achieve for them and for the firm; and what were the things that currently frustrated them about the way in which the firm was managed?

'These discussions were not only the start-up of a "getting to know you" exercise, they also highlighted the issues which the partners found frustrating. The notes from these interviews became a basic blueprint for the problems which needed to be addressed. If some of these issues could be tackled successfully early on, then the partners could feel that progress was being made and gradually develop trust in an "outsider".'

Once the management of the firm is delegated to an executive team, then this team becomes responsible for the day-to-day running of the firm. If the practice is to succeed, these leaders in turn must be willing to delegate tasks to others in a systematic way. Peter says, 'To manage any business, you need to have a sound management structure and clear lines of reporting. People need to know what their responsibilities are, who they report to and what is expected of them. It is terribly important that people have a clear understanding of what *they* have got to do within the organization.'

This equally applies to smaller firms where responsibility for running the firm rests upon fewer shoulders. Peter addresses this issue by saying, 'You've got to identify people who have natural strengths. These individuals can use these skills to help run the practice. Good management should play to individuals' strengths rather than expose their weaknesses. There is no point in giving a responsibility to a person because there is no alternative, hoping that they will get by. Apart from the likelihood of failure, it is unfair on the individual and leads to frustration and demotivation.'

Peter proposes that leaders should seek colleagues who complement their own strengths. Some leaders avoid this in fear of having their weaknesses exposed. Strong leaders and managers need the support of equally strong individuals who bring different qualities and skills to the team. Peter offers a jigsaw-like model for determining personnel who will enhance the firm by complementing its existing leaders. This model is shown here as Figure 3.2. At Gerald Eve, they use psychometric testing to assist in the recruitment process so that new practice members bring complementary skills and qualities to the team.

Ultimately, the responsibility for ensuring that the practice runs efficiently and profitably rests with the practice leaders. When there are problems, Peter says, 'You have to talk to the people who are directly affected by the problem and, by using their comments and your skills, try and identify the solution.' He suggests that by understanding these individuals' needs and fears, there is a much better chance of creating resolution: 'There is no point in imposing something on a group of people unless you genuinely understand their concerns. You've got to understand what the proposal practically entails, then succinctly explain how the solution is to be implemented.'

Field of necessary qualities

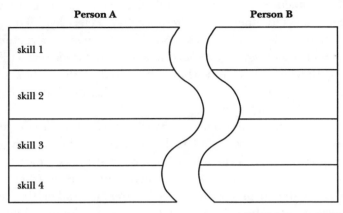

© *Haigh-Lumby, 1993*

Figure 3.2   The firm's 'big picture'.

In summing up the role and responsibilities of the manager of a practice, Peter says, 'The day-to-day work has got to be done. You have a much better chance of achieving this if you have the right people in the right places, properly trained and with appropriate experience. What you have also got to do is identify problem areas and then resolve them, while not losing sight of the "bigger picture": what is motivating the partners; where should the practice go? I do proffer a solution to this: you have got to get the balance right by being able to decide the level of an issue's importance and then devote the right resource to it. Practice management is more than just organizational details. Those in senior positions must also have a "big picture". They need a sense of vision for the practice.'

THREE APPROACHES TO LEADERSHIP

Autocratic, democratic and permissive

Effective leadership encourages both productivity and healthy professional relationships. Those leaders who listen and cooperate with their colleagues create greater success for their firms than those who dominate and limit the participation of their peers. At the beginning of this chapter, the issue of the reticent leader was discussed. An extreme alternative to this is the individual who believes that leadership means acting alone and directing affairs without consulting the partners.

In the late 1930s, Kurt Lewin, a pioneer of group dynamics, and his research associates produced a classic study of leadership behaviour. Its results were highly significant and they continue to influence ideas about effective management behaviour more than 60 years later. Although there are many contemporary management specialists who suggest that the Lewin study is out of date, in fact, its findings form the origins of interest in ideas such as 'employee empowerment', 'participative management' and 'team building initiatives'. It is interesting that the Lewin research was conducted during a period of history that is marked by the rise of dictator-led governments.

In brief, the study focused on three styles of leadership historically practised throughout organizations. The three styles were referred to as *autocratic*, *democratic* and *laissez-faire* (permissive). In the study, group leaders were trained to adopt and maintain the behaviour of one of these three styles and then guide groups of adolescents to complete tasks over a period of time.

The leadership style defined as 'autocratic', retained maximum control over goal setting and decision making and allowed minimum participation and discussion among members of the group. The 'democratic' style retained minimum control of goal setting and decision making, but the leader encouraged maximum participation and discussion within the group. The 'permissive' leader retained minimum control of goal setting and decision making and did not make any attempt to stimulate group participation and discussion.

All group leaders expressed what was called 'medium friendliness' while fulfiling their roles. This was to avoid friendliness being associated more with one style than another. This study demonstrated that leadership style produces dramatic differences in group members' behaviour.

The *permissive style* produced the least work of the poorest quality. This work was less organized and less efficient. Also, members expressed less satisfaction about their work experience when they were interviewed following their group experience.

The groups led with an *autocratic style* showed two extreme kinds of behaviour. Some members became submissive while others showed hostility, aggression, destruction and the creation of scapegoats. Although group members voiced no complaints while in the groups, they expressed considerable dissatisfaction when interviewed later.

The groups led with a *democratic style* showed equal productivity to those with an autocratic leader, but there was an important difference. Members with democratic leaders expressed three times as much genuine, spontaneous interest in *work-related* tasks when the leader left the room than did the autocratic groups. As well, members conversed about *work-related* matters much more frequently than within the democratically led groups.

One scenario, three outcomes

The following scenario describes a typical decision-making situation within a practice. Unlike real life, the managing partner has adopted only one of the three leadership styles, autocratic, democratic or permissive, in response to the scenario. Depending upon this partner's leadership style, the proposal for change can have three very different outcomes.

The scenario

In response to significant increases in professional indemnity insurance, the managing partner of a legal firm explores changing the firm's status from partnership to limited company. In the idea's favour are containment of insurance costs, limited liability for colleagues' errors and an explicit commitment to running the firm as a business. Against the idea is the potential loss of status associated with professional partnership, the displeasure of the partners and potential loss of confidence among clients who could interpret the change as an opting out of responsibility by the partners.

This managing partner is aware that there are also other associated issues, but those which immediately come to mind seem to be the most relevant. The possible outcomes of adopting one of the three leadership styles are described here.

The autocratic style

This autocratic managing partner makes a decision to change the firm's status from a partnership to a limited company. A colleague who usually agrees with this partner's choices is also consulted. This decision is then announced as definite at the next partners' meeting. Those partners who disagree find themselves on the defensive as they react to the sudden news. Their surprise and dismay leads the managing partner to suggest further analysis, but this is just a preparatory step before going ahead with the idea. Later, the issue is discussed by small groups of partners in private. Although open hostility to the idea is expressed among the partners, they have no forum established for open debate. Finally, the managing partner re-asserts authority and announces that the change will be implemented.

The democratic style

This democratic managing partner thoroughly considers the idea of changing the firm's status in private and then makes a decision about the best course of action. The purpose of this is to offer the partners a prepared analysis and a starting point for debate. It also satisfies the managing partner's personal need for clarity. The partners are given a full analysis of the proposal well in advance of a scheduled meeting so that they can fully prepare for a discussion.

Those who support or disagree are expected to present a strong case for their position. Because the proposal has such extensive implications, a vote is scheduled only after all of the partners have been heard and a complete follow-up analysis is conducted based on their input. Eventually, they decide to remain a partnership, and yet they also update virtually all of their business procedures during the process of making this decision.

The permissive style

Although the permissive managing partner originally develops the idea for changing the firm to a limited company, it is not really based on any strong views. In fact, this leader believes that 'the partners should decide' and that a good leader 'leads by following'. When the issue is raised at the next partners' meeting, the debate is fragmented and a decision is indefinitely postponed.

There are strong factions within this group of partners and decisions about even routine matters often reach deadlock. Some partners are frustrated by this, but others value the freedom and autonomy it gives them. Everyone realizes that the firm is under-performing. Even so, it seems virtually impossible to change.

Caveat

Few leaders either see or describe themselves as autocratic, even fewer as rigid, controlling and tyrannical, and certainly no one readily accepts themselves as spineless and wishy-washy. Rather, it is their peers and employees who refer to them in this way. Unfortunately, many autocratic and permissive leaders believe that they are democratic. They lack sources of direct feedback because it is their own behaviour which makes it difficult for colleagues to be honest, even if candid feedback is requested.

Only by studying the levels and standards of work achieved without supervision, the ability of practice members to collaborate and the quantity *and* quality of work-related interactions are leaders able to discover the extent of their own skill and commitment to democratic leadership. The ultimate 'acid test' for this is a firm where professionals readily debate important issues, discuss ideas and show a commitment to the firm through collaboration. This kind of firm is generally guided by a democratic leader.

Further confusion arises because an autocratic leader can also be a very nice person. In the Lewin study, all the leadership styles required 'medium friendly' behaviour. There are many benign autocrats to be found in professional situations. They retain control of goals, processes and procedures because they believe this is for their colleagues' good or is in their clients' best interest.

These leaders benefit from considering the negative results of their autocratic style. For example, within the firm it can breed submission or aggression, scapegoating and destruction. There is also a high need for autocratic leaders to provide direct supervision in order to produce successful results. In terms of client relationships, it is a style that leads to dissatisfaction, misunderstanding and a desire among intelligent and astute clients to take their business to a more receptive professional adviser.

Analysis 3

Please answer yes or no to the following questions.

	YES	NO
1 You ask your clients to clarify fully what they believe they need before advising them.	—	—
2 You encourage discussion of policy among your partners.	—	—
3 When leading meetings, you do not intervene or guide the discussion.	—	—
4 Your staff frequently express satisfaction with their work.	—	—
5 You keep people guessing about what you are going to do next.	—	—
6 Your firm has cliques and factions which ostracize those whose 'face doesn't fit'.	—	—
7 Your colleagues make their preferences known openly and spontaneously.	—	—
8 You believe that creative professionals should lead themselves.	—	—

9 Everyone knows that your favourites within the firm
receive special treatment.   —   —

10 You call a meeting to decide an urgent issue for the
practice and no one attends.   —   —

11 When you are away from the firm, its overall
productivity decreases.   —   —

12 Factions within the firm make it impossible to make
vital decisions.   —   —

Results

A *yes* answer to items:

1	2	4	7	indicates a democratic style
3	8	10	12	indicates a permissive style
5	6	9	11	indicates an autocratic style

This check-list provides an estimate of your leadership style. Only the
'yes' answers contribute to the tally because 'no' answers could indicate
one of the other two styles. For example, a 'yes' answer to item 1
indicates a democratic style. A 'no' answer could indicate either a
permissive or autocratic style. Not asking a client to clarify their
perceived requirements before giving professional advice could be the
result of either lack of direction or an unwillingness to listen.

THE ADAPTIVE LEADER

In the Gerald Eve case study (see page 55), Peter Haigh-Lumby
emphasizes democratic leadership behaviour. Although he emphasizes
debate, empowerment and delegation skills, he also takes firm decisions
when it is appropriate. The democratic style allows a leader to be
receptive and flexible and also directive and decisive. Leaders who

know how to adapt their behaviour to meet the needs of each situation provide their practice with effective management.

Categorizing leadership styles is a first step in assessing leadership behaviour. It allows individuals to consider their general behaviour and then adopt specific actions to suit varying work situations. In recent years, the management consultants Paul Hersey and Ken Blanchard proposed a model for effective leadership that is widely adopted throughout industry. Much study went into developing their system, which helps leaders decide the kind of behaviour that best serves each situation. This model suggests that groups and individuals go through a four-stage process of maturation. These stages are: 'telling', 'selling', 'participating' and 'delegating'.

Each of these stages is developmental and requires different leadership styles. Stage one begins with the group's formation. To be effective, the group needs a strong leader who tells group members what to do. The emphasis within the group is on completing tasks as well as learning work-related skills. Most interaction occurs between the leader and individual members of the group who are not yet well acquainted with each other.

Later, when the group becomes thoroughly skilled at its work, the members need a leader who aids the development of good relationships within the group. Although the completion of tasks is the reason for forming the group, the leader also wants group members to work well together. Leaders during this second phase of group maturity encourage communication among members of the group and promote mutual understanding in an effort to build good relationships.

During the third phase of maturation, group members have become both technically competent and personally comfortable within their group. The leader's task is to find a balance between encouraging good relationships and completing tasks. The members of the group can readily challenge the leader's ideas and debate key task issues among themselves toward improving their productivity and quality of work. At this stage, group members begin to participate in group leadership.

In the fourth and final stage, the members require little direction from the leader. They have become so competent and work so efficiently together that the leader has delegated completion of the group's tasks to them. Ideally, leaders of fully mature groups need only consult with members and provide general guidance about task completion.

Hersey and Blanchard call their model 'Situational Leadership'. Essentially, they suggest that leaders should evaluate the maturity of the group and its group members and then adapt their leadership behaviour to serve the needs of each situation. In principle, this is an excellent idea; in practice, it is rather difficult to achieve.

The challenge is *knowing* how to assess the level of maturity: of the group, the individual or even of the leader. If this is accurately assessed, then the leader must also know how to match the right leadership behaviour with the situation's needs. These are not easy tasks. They presuppose a considerable degree of personal insight and assume that leaders have more control over people, resources and time than they normally have in everyday work situations.

Possessing the necessary insight to manage effectively is no less a challenge within professional firms than it is in other business environments. Although professionals all have technical competence, practice leaders must identify *how much* task-related guidance is required, *for which* colleagues and *of what kind*. These decisions always rely upon personal judgement. Those professionals who do not see their own leadership shortcomings, for example, can rationalize an autocratic manner as appropriate leadership behaviour for an immature group. They can fail to recognize that it is their behaviour which impedes the group from further development.

Systems, methods and concepts are only as useful as their practitioners are self-aware. Leaders need to assess whether they have skill enough to determine when groups or individuals are fully mature, that is, ready to assume delegation of major tasks. In addition to considering issues of group maturity, leaders must also develop skills of delegation.

DELEGATION: A PRACTICE ESSENTIAL

Delegation is an essential management skill for any organization, but it is particularly valuable for professional firms. Among other benefits, it provides training for junior staff, motivates skilled associates by increasing their responsibility and frees partners to focus on assignments suited to their higher level of expertise. In spite of this, opportunities to delegate are often ignored by professionals. Partners either lack the skill to delegate successfully or the willingness to try. As well, many professionals wish to supervise all client contact personally and this technical interest overrides other considerations.

Practice leaders who emphasize the importance of delegation add stability to the firm. By encouraging associates to provide consistent back-up to partners, they gradually develop not only technical expertise, but also build relationships with clients themselves. Some partners find this threatening because they fear that *their* clients will be taken over by junior members of the firm. This risk is offset by an increase in service continuity for the client. When partners encourage delegation, they need also to discourage colleagues from poaching each others' clients.

A convincing case should be made for delegation so that its benefits to the firm are obvious. A way to encourage partners to delegate routine and administration tasks to more junior members of a practice, is to agree to a budget for time spent by partners for this kind of work. When partners accept an appropriate minimum budget and also realize that delegation frees them to pursue client work, they more readily accept this as an essential professional skill.

Delegation guides experienced associates to assume responsibility for higher level work. This serves both the individual and the firm. While engaging the young professional's interest, delegation also prepares the firm for emergencies. If associates are kept in the dark about critical assignments, they are unable to substitute for a partner in the event of an emergency.

The long-term viability of the firm depends upon developing the next generation of partners. The most talented among the associates need assurance that the firm offers them career development prospects; otherwise, they will seek better opportunities elsewhere. The delegation of interesting and challenging assignments is a powerful inducement to keep the best of the next generation within the firm.

The delegation process

When delegation is used correctly, it offers a means for systematically training junior staff; by challenging their skills, building confidence and inspiring them to greater achievement. A relevant and related issue concerns the risk involved in trusting less experienced members of a firm with clients' assignments. There are partners who pay lip-service to the *idea* of delegation, but resist its actual *practice*. These leaders authorize their delegatees to complete tasks and yet watch their every movement toward anticipating possible mistakes.

The common rationalization for this behaviour is the wish to ensure that the client gets the best service, but delegatees justifiably resent this style of burdensome supervision. Although powerless to complain, the most promising among them eventually seek greater challenge elsewhere

In addition to personnel issues, intense supervision also creates an ethical dilemma. If excessive time is spent in supervision, the delegating partner actually bills the client twice for the same work. While this means a short-term financial gain for the firm, it could also lead to the long-term loss of the client's business. Clients who believe they are being consistently over-charged, tend to take their business elsewhere.

This dilemma can be solved by ensuring that all of the partners and practice managers know how to delegate effectively. Many professionals learn this skill by trial and error. They blend common sense and experience. Sometimes this works and at other times it does not. Although they would like to be more systematic, they are far too busy to research and develop a delegation method for themselves. This results in professionals believing that their delegation is effective only to hear from their colleagues that it is not.

Delegation empowers another person to decide how to complete a task. Projects that require extensive instruction and constant supervision are either unsuited to delegation or are assigned to the wrong person. Once the task is assigned, supervision should occur at a distance. If it does not, this is interference, not delegation.

The delegation process includes the following stages:

- defining the task clearly
- presenting its importance and how it fits into the firm's other activities
- explaining the degree of authority granted and the accountability for end results
- monitoring and evaluating progress at agreed intervals.

Defining the task

Because this step is so obvious, it is often given least attention, particularly if clear goals are set for task completion. Even so, the limits of each specific task should be outlined, and ideas sought from delegatees about how best to complete the task. Those who are delegated responsibility feel empowered when they have helped decide what the task includes. This decision is then summarized in a few written sentences to be kept by both the project leader and the person who is delegated the task. Any changes to the assignment are then added to these notes. This not only provides a basis for evaluating performance, but also contributes valuable information to a final summary of the project. This process is often called 'creating ownership'. Good delegators encourage people to feel responsible for the success of their work, so that they 'own' its achievement themselves.

Presenting the reason for its importance

'Possessive ownership' is avoided when time is also taken to explain how the task contributes to other assignments, to the project itself and to the whole practice. Providing an overview perspective or a 'big picture' encourages understanding, interest and involvement. The junior people on the team appreciate this most. It is a sign that the boss takes them seriously and wants them to understand the importance of their job. This explanation is best given when they are first assigned the task because it may influence any suggestions they offer regarding its completion.

Explaining their authority and accountability

This step includes describing the kind and amount of responsibility delegatees are given to complete the task. The limit of their authority is also explained as well as the circumstances under which they should seek advice before making decisions. This implies that they are also told when, where and how they can reach an adviser for this support. Delegators create serious problems, if not crises, when they delegate and then simply disappear. This is the opposite of over-supervision. Although a different problem, it is equally frustrating to be on its receiving end. It also seriously jeopardizes the success of the project.

Delegatees want clear performance standards and information about how the task will be evaluated. This removes ambiguity, a major cause of stress at work. If questions are encouraged at the beginning of the task, the answers clarify what successful completion looks like for this assignment.

Monitoring and evaluating progress

This step refers to the leaders' ultimate responsibility for the completed task. If progress is monitored effectively, there is a double yield: the work is done and the delegatee has a sense of achievement with minimal risk to the project's success. If expectations have been explained in advance, then the harsh edge of criticism is removed at the project's completion.

When delegatees know their requirements in advance and actually help to define them, there is a sense of fairness in the evaluation. When the task's outcome is discussed in terms of prearranged targets, delegatees can be given direct feedback without loss of morale, hurt feelings or complaint. This is critique of a specific performance, not of the person.

It is also important to give recognition when it is due. Even when there are weak achievement areas, it is important to find at least one strength and say this aloud. Too often managers say, 'They know what they did well. I don't need to say so.' This is a mistaken view. Positive feedback is not only a way to reassure colleagues, it also provides an example of the kind of performance that is valued. When people have clear performance standards, they can choose to modify their behaviour to meet them.

Risk management

Following these guidelines provides risk management for delegation. It is important that delegatees know what is expected of them. Too often, failure is the result of poor communication and sketchy descriptions of the requirements of task. The task should be explained so that the delegatees recognize its importance and understand the limits of their own authority. The delegator can then watch from the sidelines and be available when needed to guide the project at critical junctures.

It can seem contradictory that this approach includes the step of 'monitoring and evaluation' while also emphasizing independence. In fact, this step is a vital one when delegation is used to educate junior members. If they are told in advance when and how their performance will be assessed, they can set clear goals for themselves. Later, when their work is evaluated, they can assess their own performance as well. When criteria for success are available, all members of a firm more readily accept critiques of their work.

The form shown in Figure 3.3, provides a guide for encouraging delegation. Partners can use this to record the purpose and outcome of delegating tasks to their associates and juniors. A separate sheet should be kept for each delegatee. Partners improve their awareness of what and how they delegate by regularly reviewing their delegatees' performance.

MOTIVATION

A firm's success depends upon its professionals' willingness to use their expertise in service of clients' needs. The attitude and commitment which they bring to the practice are important because their skill provides the firm's sole source of revenue. If the members of a practice lack the motivation to achieve results, serve clients or contribute their best effort, then the practice suffers. Although ambition and a desire

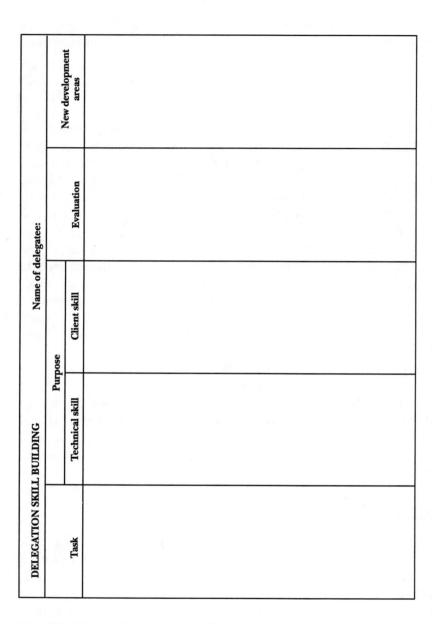

Figure 3.3   Managing delegation: a sample form.

for achievement are personal attributes, practice leaders can also influence their colleagues so that they perform better.

This skill often depends upon understanding what each professional considers a suitable reward for an excellent performance. This can vary from receipt of professional recognition, to money, status, job satisfaction, or feelings of altruistic service. Motivation is linked to meaning and purpose. Individuals bring a greater will to their work when they believe that there is a meaningful end result.

For example, there are professionals who are driven by a need to influence others' lives for the better. Within the same firm, there are others whose prime motive is the pursuit of a large income. Every profession includes these extremes of behaviour. Theories which explain, in very general terms, the nature of human motivation are often less helpful when dealing with specific individuals who need encouragement to achieve their best work.

This is a challenging issue because often people do not know what they want or even recognize their own expectations until they are not met. To illustrate this, refer to the example of a highly talented and skilled professional who is invited to become a partner. Because all of the partners have private secretaries, he imagines that he will receive private secretarial support as well. Although he receives a better office and many perquisites, he discovers that he must continue to request support from the secretarial pool as he did when he was an associate.

When he tactfully queries this situation, the managing partner laughs, never imagining the seriousness of the request. Six months later, this newly appointed partner leaves the firm having been recruited by a rival practice. The managing partner is very surprised and never actually learns the reason for his colleague's departure.

Practice leaders cannot be mind-readers and yet they have to deal effectively with their colleagues' expectations. When circumstances require that hopes are disappointed, then an explanation should be offered. Otherwise, colleagues feel demotivated and let down to a greater extent than is necessary. Regular contact with colleagues encourages communication and the development of understanding about what motivates them, professionals and non-professionals. The firm benefits from a flexible incentive programme which actively seeks information about what people want to receive, accomplish and experience through their working life.

Motivation enhances performance because it causes individuals to exert additional effort. Any number of incentives can be offered to stimulate motivation, but without an initial act of will to perform well, they are all wasted. Professionals choose to exert effort not just once when they join the firm, but daily as and when they use their expertise. Their lives are a series of acts of will because the very nature of professional work requires beginning again for each case or project.

Practice leaders who recognize this can make their colleagues' point of choice making and commitment to work easier by affirming achievement and success within the firm openly and publicly. This, of course, is a stimulant for those who seek recognition. More important, though, it is also a way to establish successful achievement as the standard behaviour within the firm. Open affirmation of a project's completion even if its success is limited signals the importance of effort and commitment to the firm.

Earlier in this chapter reference was made to Kurt Lewin's research work on leadership style. In an earlier study, he also proposed that individuals seek goals which they believe to be attainable. Furthermore, the members of a group of high-achieving peers not only influence their immediate circle to aspire to challenging goals, but also everyone within a wider range of contact. Seeing what others can attain actually causes individuals to set higher goals for themselves.

Mentoring

When achievement is openly acknowledged, this establishes a climate of success and excitement throughout the firm. For some firms, the public recognition of individual achievement can seem inappropriate. In this case, practice leaders should employ other ways to communicate and affirm success within their firm. One method which serves a variety of professional styles is to formalize the practice of mentoring.

This method assigns younger and less-established professionals to specific senior-level advisors. In regular one-to-one meetings, the junior hears about the achievements of the partner. Stories of success and failure are recounted so that junior members learn not only professional technique, but also the kind of behaviour that is associated with success. Mentoring is an excellent means for motivating both senior and junior members within the firm.

Career development

Creating a plan for professional and personal development is another way to encourage colleagues' motivation. This applies to senior as well as junior members of a firm. Development of professional goals and a commitment to their achievement enhances the completion of current projects and cases. One essential motivator for highly accomplished people is the need to create meaning and purpose in their lives. By linking daily activities to the accomplishment of long-term goals, routine activities gain greater significance.

It is unlikely that any individual has achieved all that he or she has wished within their careers. Taking time to evaluate achievement and plan for further development allows discovery of new qualities and new ambitions. This is particularly relevant for senior-level members of a firm. Also, when colleagues experience periods of self-doubt or introspection as a result of personal or professional crisis, career development encourages them to use this phase to its best advantage.

For younger firm members, a career plan adds to their enthusiasm for the completion of each project. Each achievement indicates increasing success. This not only fires their careers, but has an impact on their colleagues' motivation and goal setting. Each publicized achievement contributes to motivate other practice members to achieve their career goals as well. This returns to the idea that high achievers inspire high goal setting among their colleagues.

There are no *good reasons* to be silent about a colleague's success. It is up to the firm's leadership to find an appropriate way to promote practice achievements throughout the firm. This effort contributes to the creation of highly motivated and inspired professionals without practice leaders 'trying to be inspiring' by themselves. Like 'trying to be funny' such an effort all too often fails. Wiser leaders allow their democratically led colleagues to inspire each other to the firm's material benefit.

PROBLEM – ANALYSIS – DISCUSSION

Problem

A legal firm in the United States had 300 partners when it filed for protection against creditors in New York Bankruptcy Court. As the firm's partners sought other jobs and its employees queued for their final salary payments, the once-respected, 150-year-old firm ceased operation. This was a firm which had prospered during the boom, growth years of the 1980s. Based in an important north-eastern city, its international client list and wide range of specialisms ensured lucrative and substantial dealings. The original firm grew by absorbing small, respected, specialist firms, including those in other cities. Five years before the firm's closure, nominal control of its network of ten firms rested with the managing partner. To support him a managing board was established which included a leading member from each of the absorbed firms.

The pressure of client work and the need to manage business within the individual firms soon reduced the time available for the board members to meet. Concerned that communication and decision making would suffer, they hired a non-lawyer to act as an executive chairman, responsible for the firm's overall management.

Although the firm's legal status as a partnership was clearly defined, other critical issues were left unresolved. The newly hired executive chairman began by analysing the firm's ten separate business plans, their ten different financial record-keeping systems, as well as assessing the very different management styles expressed in each of these subdivisions. He discovered that the 300 partners had only one behaviour in common. They were all permissive about fee collection preferring to leave this task until the last two months of each fiscal year.

His analysis also highlighted the fact that the firm lacked any provision for accumulating capital. Each year, the partners looked forward to doubling their annual salaries with profit-sharing. These profits were determined by an elaborate formula linked to the equity each firm held when it merged with the original firm. The executive chairman identified serious potential problems with this system.

He was also aware that many of the firm's clients were heading for financial trouble: prominent companies were going into liquidation, others were suffering severe cash problems and those still successful were providing the firm with far less business. As three successive financial quarters showed a growing loss, the executive chairman worked to convince the partners that the firm was in crisis.

Unfortunately, his requests for action were largely ignored: primarily because the partners knew from experience that their finances always came right at year-end, and also because they believed his alarm arose from a lack of familiarity with managing a prestigious law firm. At year-end, the executive chairman presented a proposal for reform while also announcing that there were no profits and a dramatically increased overdraft. After hours of discussion, the board resolved to fire the executive chairman and resume managing the firm themselves.

During the next year, little action was taken and highly skilled and well-known partners began to seek positions elsewhere. Towards the following year-end, a disagreement took place in public between two partners about shared responsibility for the firm's debt. Unfortunately, this was publicized in the press just as a core group of partners approached the bank for a substantial loan. The loan was refused and the firm was asked to begin overdraft reduction immediately. Four months later, the firm filed for bankruptcy.

Analysis

1   With hindsight, what should the firm have done to avert this disaster?

2   What kind of leadership was appropriate for this firm:

- during the boom years
- after firing the executive chairman
- for developing its future plans?

3   How could the executive chairman have gained the partners' confidence?

4   What potential advantage could be found in the unfortunate publicity?

Discussion

This firm's leaders behaved as if leadership and the direction of their firm did not matter. They created growth by acquiring other firms and yet made no attempt to integrate business systems or management styles. The extent of the disaster is in direct proportion to the permissiveness of the firm's board of partners.

Their critical error was hiring an executive chairman to manage the firm on their behalf and then ignoring his advice out of bias and self-delusion. If they did not believe that a non-lawyer could manage their firm, they should have hired a lawyer for the post. Instead, they chose a leader from whom they withheld support. The end result was a vacuum where the management should have been.

A democratic attitude to leadership is always wise, and yet, as management situations vary, this ideal requires adaptation. During the firm's boom years, its leaders should have set clear goals and guidelines for integrating the newly merged firms and partners. This phase should have been followed by much discussion and encouraged collaboration until the firm gradually adopted a common direction and unified management system.

When the partners hired the executive chairman, they would have gained most benefit by giving him their confidence and listening to his advice. Because they were unwilling to do either, they fired him. Having done so, their next step should at least have been to fill the leadership gap themselves with strong direction, practice promotion, communication throughout the firm and a resolve to inspire confidence among lenders. Instead, they fought among themselves and drifted closer to eventual failure. To develop future plans credible to a bank manager, the firm's leaders needed to demonstrate an end to poor management and a willingness to make sound decisions for the future. They chose instead to seek further loans to maintain current spending.

The exiting executive chairman needed diplomacy and tact to win allies to his view of the firm. It was his job to convince the partners that they faced a financial crisis *different* from those of previous years. This would have been possible if expert, legitimate and influential power sources had been managed wisely.

Finally, the unfavourable publicity could have been used by the core group of partners to rally support within the firm. An outside enemy can be a gift to leaders when their colleagues are in disarray. However, it can also mean certain defeat if those leaders do not know how to inspire, guide or influence.

SUMMARY

This chapter emphasizes the importance of the relationship between leaders and followers, suggesting that they are mutually dependent roles. A definition of leadership is also proposed. Four kinds of power are defined and it is suggested that leaders should not only acknowledge their power, but also exercise choice about what kind of power they use. Three approaches to leadership are described, autocratic, democratic and permissive, and the democratic approach is recommended as by far the most effective. It is also proposed that leaders adapt their behaviour to suit each management situation. This leads to a discussion of a four-step process for delegation and techniques for motivating colleagues at work.

4

Vision and planning

THE POWER OF INSPIRATION

An inspiring vision can stimulate more interest and commitment than promises of money, status or power, and it also serves as a powerful influence when difficult decisions must be faced. Discussions about vision lead to better understanding of colleagues' values and their sources of motivation. Although a firm can exist without articulating a vision, its expression creates the possibility of united, practice-wide effort. Clarity and agreement within a partnership encourages wholesome and positive action. This is a powerful contributor to practice success.

The creation of a vision requires partners to integrate their individual hopes, dreams and wishes so that individual goals are balanced with the need for collaboration. A vision statement makes explicit the purpose of the partnership which, in turn, guides the development of specific goals for the practice. Partners who commit themselves to this process lay the foundation for efficient decision making. This is because a shared vision provides criteria for assessing the best options for their firm.

Because professionals already ascribe to the vision and ethical code of their professional association, it would seemingly be a small step to develop a vision for their firms, and yet this task is highly challenging. Vision requires a response to the question, 'What do I want the future to hold?' This means creating images for a positive outcome, fruitful development and worthy enterprise *before* any effort is made to achieve these. Vision is the first stage of transforming pure potential into actuality. The process of developing vision is not and never actually should be easy.

CASE STUDY: JOHNS HOPKINS UNIVERSITY WILLIAM H. WELCH MEDICAL LIBRARY

The purpose of this case study is to highlight the importance of developing a vision. The professional whose views are presented here argues the necessity for vision, its specific advantages and proposes a method for developing it. She also illustrates through her own work how that vision contributes to success by serving as a guide for action.

Nina Matheson is Professor of Medical Information and Director of the Johns Hopkins University William H. Welch Medical Library. This library is considered one of the leaders in the application of computer technologies to the management of published medical information and on-line databases. Nina has influenced the organization of health sciences libraries and the development of medical information management projects throughout the US, Europe and Asia through her writings and through the example of the Library which she leads.

She suggests that innovation and change in tradition-bound professions such as medicine and librarianship require robust vision and commitment to turn that vision into reality through strategic planning and reallocation of resources. She says, 'It's vision that rallies people, that causes them to see their own self-interest in the larger cause and long-term goals. Articulating a compelling vision is the hardest thing to do, but I consider my job to think big and to push the process of change. The electronic technologies are transforming all of our lives, as we know, but they are so fundamental to the work of libraries and the health and biological sciences that we must take charge of and direct that change. But, it is hard for people to tell you what they want when they don't have any concept of what technologies can actually do.'

Not only does a vision for the future enable her professional colleagues to accept innovation, but it also helps them to define it. 'I've discovered that people need a picture into which they can place themselves. Once they can imagine how they might do things differently, or do different things, the barriers to pursuing the vision begin to break down. When I first came to Hopkins eight years ago, I talked a great deal about the technologies and how they could transform medical libraries and create "knowledge workstations". People's eyes would glaze over after two minutes. Finally, one very wise adviser said, 'Just tell me what this is going to do for me and how these things are going to help me." I realized then that people aren't interested in changing the library. They are interested in getting more of what they want and need from their library. They aren't interested in the technologies *per se*, or processes and techniques, but in results. My role was to collaborate with them to create the vision of how they will work in the future and then set about making that vision a reality as soon as possible.'

If vision is to engage the support of fellow professionals, it must have goals beyond some immediate, short-term self-interest. Each step, each project, must add up and lead to some significant goals. Vision serves three different levels:

1   to resolve a specific problem or need
2   to answer bigger questions about the firm's overall and long-term needs
3   to make a major contribution to society's needs.

While the vision is crucial, the translation into reality depends upon strategic thinking and planning. In this way, Nina's ideas have direct application to professional firms. Hard decisions have to be made in terms of resources and their allocation because in few cases are additional resources readily available. The projects that are implemented need to feed into and dovetail with a larger overall strategy. Otherwise resources may be wasted, opportunities lost or expectations not met. Meeting expectations is critical.

CREATING A VISION

Although there are inspired individuals who seem able to see their future unfold in advance of events, as Nina Matheson describes, most people are challenged to create a vision. Only by repeatedly asking, 'What do I really want and what actions should I take to achieve this?' do they gradually develop vision, purpose and direction. This questioning process is even more challenging when there are several individuals working to create a common vision. Partners frequently discover that they each have different ideas about the firm's future. This is natural because, as individuals, they have different points of view and even professional interests. Even so, these contradictions must be resolved or the firm unavoidably becomes divided.

Differences of vision are a major cause of partnership break-up, and this situation is exacerbated by a generally experienced inability to identify fragmented vision as the main source of partners' friction. This lack of awareness makes it impossible to discuss deeply felt differences openly and directly. The cause, at least in part, is often due to partners having focused exclusively on personal and professional similarities at the outset of their partnership. The features and behaviour they *seemed* to have in common were considered to be the basis for a good working relationship.

Although this approach makes common sense, it leads to surprise when strong differences eventually emerge. Later, when attempting to resolve these differences, partners frequently focus on their initial expectations of each other in an effort to discover 'what went wrong'. This approach inevitably leads to recrimination and possible bad feeling. In fact, nothing 'went wrong', rather new professional priorities *always* emerge as partners' interests change and develop over time.

An alternative approach for resolving differences of priorities suggests that partners explore the root cause of their difficulties. This is achieved by discussing their *current needs*, their *evolving vision* and, as a result, the *priorities* they believe are *currently* appropriate to them as individuals. Focusing on present differences, rather than past expecta-tions and assumed similarities, opens up the debate about the firm's future and legitimizes individual needs.

The first step to resolving differences is to acknowledge that partners have the right to experience them. This is far from fatal to the practice. Because it is only natural that some features of each partner's hopes and ambitions contradict those of their colleagues, making these differences explicit actually strengthens the likelihood of compromise and mutual acceptance. Refusal to disclose personal preferences blocks communication and makes eventual agreement impossible.

When partners finally do agree to a practice vision, then managing the firm's resources becomes easier. Because staff and non-partner professionals have information about the firm's goals and priorities, this allows them to act more effectively on the partners' behalf. Sincere and committed people want to pull in a common direction. They do not like working in an environment where there is endless, even acrimonious, debate about practice priorities.

Staff contribute more to a practice when its leaders tell them where it is going and invite them to suggest better ways of getting there. There is certainly enough research available to convince even the most cynical professional that people want and need to feel involved in their work. Contributing ideas which benefit the firm's future is virtually impossible if the future is never discussed. As well, it is unrealistic to ask staff to offer suggestions if partners do not know how to integrate good ideas into a plan or how to refuse any impractical ideas tactfully.

Particularly when finances make a firm's future seem uncertain, discussion about practice vision helps focus on the firm's long-term needs. Nina Matheson's work in the field of information management is successful, at least in part, because she asks clients first to consider vision and then to seek the best possible solution to their present problems. When they have expressed their wishes and requirements for the future, this allows the development of a plan of action. As technology continues to advance, the vision these clients develop guides any further innovations. Without the direction which vision provides, change is random and isolated, and opportunities are lost.

Analysis 4

This analysis is in two parts. Part 1 should be completed by individuals without reference to the opinions of their colleagues. Part 2 serves as a discussion guide for colleagues who wish to reach mutual agreement about their practice vision.

Part 1: *individuals*

1 What qualities do you bring to the partnership (list at least three)?

2 What qualities do each of your partners bring (list at least three for each partner)?

3 Do you believe the firm as a whole has certain qualities? If so, what are they?

4 What do you want your professional life to be like in five years' time?

5 What would life in the ideal professional firm be like *for you*?

6 Identify and make notes about any gaps between your answers to questions 4 and 5 and the present reality of your professional life?

Part 2: *group discussion*

Participants need two hours for discussion of their answers to the questions in Part 1. If the group is larger than eight, then smaller groups should be formed for discussion. A discussion leader should be chosen for each group.

The discussion best takes place in a quiet location without interruption. Participants should sit so that everyone can see the others (please refer to 'Rich' communication, page 206). A flip chart, paper and pens are also needed.

1 Each person first shares the answers to questions 1 and 2 from Part 1. A general discussion should be discouraged at this stage.

2 Answers to question 3 are shared and written on a flip chart so that everyone in the group can see any repetitions and differences.

3 Each person then shares their answers to questions 4 and 5. The leader ensures that interruptions are kept to a minimum so that participants each have a chance to describe their own ideals.

4 Question 6 of Part 1 marks the starting point for general debate. The focus for this discussion is the discovery of what participants want the future to hold as well as how they currently describe their

firm. Key ideas should be written on flip chart paper, then later typed and distributed to the partners. These notes form the basis for the group's next discussion.

Additional two-hour sessions should be scheduled until the partners develop a shared vision for the firm. Where serious differences emerge, adequate time should be given for resolving these.

THE MISSION STATEMENT

A mission statement is a short written summary of the partners' shared vision for the future. The debate about vision is the first step in the process of developing this for the practice. There can be some resistance to producing a mission statement at first because popular belief associates it with the management of large corporations. Many professionals further equate it with a slick company slogan, such as 'We are first and best'. This caricature undermines the mission statement's function of providing an organization with a clear statement of its intent and purpose.

In fact, a professional practice benefits considerably from formulating a mission statement. Because firms feel the effects of economic turbulence, demographic shift and social change just as keenly as do other businesses in the community, partners need to create stability. They develop this by considering the firm's future, making a commitment to achieve a common purpose and then working towards it together. In this way, the partners prepare themselves for unified action in the event of difficulties. A mission statement is a major step toward ensuring the firm's long-term viability.

To have validity, though, it must be based upon the partners' vision. The practice mission functions as a means to inspire commitment from everyone who works within the firm. Otherwise, it is a waste of time, a cliché and the empty slogan of popular belief. Although there are several ways to write a mission statement, certain information is essential. This includes stating the legal status of the practice, its purpose, primary commitment and general goals for the next five years in just two or three short sentences. For example, the mission statement for a hypothetical medical practice in the UK could read like this:

> **The Nelson Crescent Surgery is a general practice partnership formed to provide health care to NHS patients. Its dedicated partners have a primary commitment to give excellent, conscientious and timely medical care to NHS list patients and also include research pursuits and private patients as additional surgery activities.**

Implied in this statement is an agreement among the surgery's four partners to work within the NHS while allowing two of the team to conduct research, and the other two to treat some patients privately. These decisions emerge as a result of hours of discussion, weeks of soul-searching and some heated debate. The partners must first clarify their vision for the future and then summarize this into the practical requirements of a mission statement. The time and energy expended for this is an investment in the long-term success of the practice.

A well-produced and accurate mission statement binds its producers to mutual support of individual and collective activity. The more commitment that is brought into producing the mission statement, then the more likely that it expresses the partners' most profoundly felt ambitions. When personal will is harnessed to the practice in this way, individuals bring enormous reserves of energy to their work.

As well, a practice mission ends the repeated discussion of basic practice issues. Decisions become easier because the principals have already agreed to a general direction for the practice. In the hypothetical case of Nelson Crescent Surgery, potential resentment about private patients or time taken for research is dispersed when these considerations are fully debated and then integrated into the mission statement.

Alternatively, these doctors could decide that research is a project for pursuit outside of surgery hours or that private patients are not to be treated. In that case, the principals would decide an appropriate compromise which would satisfy all four of them. The essential point is to integrate their individual goals and priorities within the mission statement and then make decisions about ongoing practice business in harmony with this agreement. The increased clarity of purpose which follows allows increased efficiency. As well, the inclusion of personal goals improves professional relationships within the practice. Firms with a mission have an advantage over every one of their competitors who have not examined their common purpose.

Ambiguity is a major cause of tension at work. Clear guidelines from the firm's leaders allow everyone to produce better work with less stress. When people know the firm's priorities, then they can contribute more readily to them. It is surprising how many professional firms, commercial enterprises and government agencies still believe that basic information about the firm should be given on 'a need to know basis'. This ignores the fact that people who only partially know what is expected of them can only partially perform. They cannot give 100 per cent because they can never be fully assured that they are engaged in the right activities.

Writing a mission statement

A mission statement should serve a firm for at least five years. At first, this can seem a very long period of time to consider in advance. Actually, partners who allow themselves to dream about the future in preparation for writing their mission statement soon recognize that five years is a very short span of time. The mission statement gives a direction to practice activity, rather than presents highly detailed goals. Even if this task seems challenging, the discipline of thinking ahead prepares partners for making future decisions. Paradoxically, planning actually allows a more flexible response to changing circumstances.

The written statement generally takes the form of a 30- to 50-word summary of a firm's long-term aims and objectives. The best of these briefly describes the 'who, what, when, where, and how' of the firm in positive and even inspiring terms. The following three statements provide examples of company missions. They are taken from actual firms, with their details altered in order to maintain confidentiality.

Our mission is to operate in the following markets: building, construction, containers and long-haul delivery.

Our products are the best and we put our clients first. We aim to provide all employees with job security, work satisfaction, training and above-average remuneration.

Our mission is to finance internal growth from a percentage of our profits.

Although all three of these statements meet the criterion of brevity, they lack other more vital mission statement features. As well, all three are potentially confusing to anyone not involved in their development and certainly not one of them inspires.

For example, the first describes the firm's mission in terms of 'markets', then offers a list of business activities, not markets. The second leaves the reader guessing what kind of products the firm offers while asserting that they are the best. It also poses a potential contradiction because, at times, putting the client first means curtailment of employees' job satisfaction. Finally, the third is a masterpiece of ambiguity. The reader is left to imagine the meaning of 'internal growth', the proportion of profit it is to receive and even what the firm produces.

It is interesting that the developers of these mission statements put considerable effort into them and yet fall far short of a successful outcome. They would have been wiser to begin by reaching an agreement about their *collective vision* and then basing their mission statement upon that. All three examples rely on factual statements only. They lack imagination, a sense of direction and the capacity to cause a reader to say, 'What a good idea.' If the company leaders depend upon these statements to inspire their colleagues to contribute their best effort to the firm, they are in serious trouble.

At issue, then, is whether ordinary people can write a mission statement, and, if so, who should be part of the team which produces it? This is a topic of continual debate among management theorists, but here, it is proposed that the *only* people who should produce a mission statement are those who need to use and refer to it themselves. Slick, professional efforts cannot reflect the vision of the people responsible for the firm. It is this harnessing of vision that gives a mission statement meaning. Having said this, there are a few guidelines which benefit the production of an inspiring mission and also help avoid some of the difficulties which can attend the process.

The first of these is to limit the development team to those who actually take *ultimate responsibility* for the firm. In a partnership, this is most obviously the partners themselves. Exceptions can be made as long as these are based upon the person's long-term commitment to the practice. It is a nonsense to attempt to include the hopes and dreams of people only temporarily involved with the firm. Anyone who contributes to a mission statement should also be fully committed to working towards its goals until they are achieved, legally, ethically, morally and financially. Those who own the firm or who are its legal and financial guardians are the appropriate developers of its mission statement.

Having proposed this, it must also be added that staff input is extremely valuable for improving virtually every aspect of business life. There are leaders who recognize this and so wish to include their long-term staff and non-partner professionals in the process of writing the firm's mission statement. They see this as an invitation to take an active part in the firm. This decision serves some firms very well, but caution recommends that partners first produce a strong first draft.

This is necessary because the larger the group engaged in writing a mission statement, the longer the process takes and the less dynamic the end result is likely to be. Inevitably, some contributors feel disappointed because their 'key words' are not included. If staff are to be included in producing the mission statement, they should be told in advance the limits of their influence on the process. The basic idea is to encourage participation, but to avoid the implication that the final wording is a matter for democratic vote.

This caveat for a small drafting group also applies to firms with a large number of partners. A small, representative team should draft a mission statement and then invite the general partnership to make comments and offer suggestions. This can be time-consuming, and yet if the partners' vision for the firm has been explored first, the representative group bases their effort on this information.

Alternatively, there are those who believe that a mission statement should be written in full by a single leader on behalf of everyone else and then announced to the partners in general. This approach is of debatable value if the purpose of producing a mission statement is for partners to reach agreement about their future and to reaffirm commitment to their partnership. As well, in today's complex society, it is unlikely that a single individual can bring the degree of perception and strategic thinking which an entire team of partners brings to the process.

Once the composition of the group is decided, the members should begin to define the firm's mission in terms of:

who:
- a statement of the firm's legal status
- the people who provide the service
- the population targeted to receive the service

what:
- the nature of the firm's products and services

when:
- the sense of timing the firm brings to delivery of its products and services

where:
- the geographical area or country in which the firm focuses its activity

how:
- the quality of the firm's products and services
- the firm's financial goals and ambitions.

The discussion of these issues is considerably eased if the partners have already reached agreement about their shared vision for the practice. Analysis 4 on pages 84 to 86 asks partners to consider their individual qualities as well as those of the firm overall. Examining qualities in this way contributes directly to creating an inspiring and authentic mission statement because this draws upon what is most deeply felt by the partners.

Definition of terms

Having produced a brief mission statement, the partners should examine it yet again. If there are any generalities or ambiguous terms, these should be defined so that all the partners agree. Phrases such as, 'quality first', 'the best' or 'leaders in the profession', are all subject to individual interpretation. They are certainly suitable for inclusion in a mission statement as long as the partners know *exactly what they mean* among themselves.

These definitions should be written down for future reference. They also provide partners with a basis for setting specific objectives when they formulate a plan for the practice. For example, if the partners of a firm of construction engineers believe that 'quality first' means receiving British Standard 5750 (see page 39), then this requires the achievement of a set of objectives associated with gaining BS 5750 approval. Clarity about what the partners mean by 'quality' makes them aware of the more specific issues which must be decided toward accomplishing that goal.

On the other hand, highly detailed definitions of terms detract from the impact of a short, sharp and inspiring mission statement. A frequently used solution is the publication of a brief mission. This is followed by definitions and a list of the specific objectives associated with the mission statement for in-house use. Because some of the objectives are likely to be confidential, they are not for outside publication. Obviously, staff and non-partner professionals within the firm are given this information; otherwise, they cannot contribute fully to achieving the mission.

SETTING GOALS

As soon as any discussion moves from the abstract to the concrete, partners automatically shift their attention from producing a mission statement to creating a plan of action. For example, a mission can include the phrase, 'We offer comprehensive advice'. This leads partners to discuss how their practice best provides this. Several options are then proposed, from recruiting specialist advisors to subscribing to international database services. Finally, the partners make concrete and specific choices so that their promise to offer comprehensive advice is fulfilled.

These concrete choices form the basis of a practice plan. When plans directly result from an examination of vision and mission statement, then they are based on the planners' actual preferences, past experiences and available resources. As well, partners are more highly motivated to achieve the plan's goals because they obviously lead to the achievement of their ambitions. The following example illustrates the natural development of goals as they emerge from a professional firm's mission statement. The mission reads:

> **We are a Stockholm-based partnership of architects providing international leadership in commercial and industrial design. Beauty, a respect for human requirements and scrupulous attention to detail underlie all of our work.**

This statement is a summary of the firm's long-term goals. It serves the partners by:

- reaffirming their home base of Stockholm
- limiting their design projects to commercial and industrial work
- stating publicly their three ideals of beauty, commitment to their clients' needs and the provision of quality work
- announcing their world-wide markets and leadership in the field.

The production of this mission requires that the partners agree to definitions for certain key words. These are:

- **Stockholm-based partnership of architects**

  This is a statement of fact. They have only one office and they do not wish to open others or licence other firms to use their firm's name. These phrases clarify their intentions, but do not generate any new goals.

- **international leadership**

  When the partners define what this means to them, specific goals emerge about how they can maintain and further enhance their current reputation. They also set new goals for future bids and award competitions.

- **commercial and industrial design**

This harmless-looking phrase is the result of weeks of heated debate. It signals the partners' decision to refuse residential design and local government contracts. These projects are seen to require far more effort than their financial return justifies. Some partners strongly believe that no professional firm should ever refuse work. Gradually, as they reach accord, goals emerge for gaining new business in defined specialist areas and slowly withdrawing from present activity in non-specialist areas.

- **beauty**

These partners share most agreement for the meaning of this term. Their unity helps them to reaffirm their commitment to partnership, particularly because it was an agreement about aesthetics which originally drew them together to form their firm. They develop goals for continued personal and professional development and for partners' individual study of world-wide architectural achievements.

- **concern for human requirements**

This phrase leads the partners to decide that they need to improve their knowledge of new developments in ergonomics (the study of the physical environment's impact upon human efficiency). They set a goal of recruiting a specialist in this field.

- **scrupulous care**

The firm is in pursuit of International Standard 9000 (see BS 5750, page 39). They are committed to quality for its own sake and yet also want to advertise this through receipt of official recognition. Goals emerge to continue this process.

Strategy development

The architects' development of a mission statement allows them to define a general direction for the growth of the practice and to identify long-term goals. To achieve this, they also need a strategy so that they concentrate their effort toward fulfilling their ambitions. Strategy addresses the following three questions:

- Where are we now?
- Where do we want to go?
- How do we plan to get there?

The first two of these questions are summarized in the mission statement, or at least they should be. The third is addressed by developing a plan of action. When plans fill the gap between 'where we are now' and 'where we want to go', they are most likely to be implemented because they serve the partners' expressed wishes.

The five business areas

Every organization includes five general areas of business activity. These are mutually dependent and interrelated so that any development or change to one business area has an impact on the others (see Figure 4.1). These five areas are:

- people
- products and services
- finance
- facilities
- marketing.

Definitions of each are:

- **people**   This area refers to both professional and non-professional staff members within the firm as well as the administrative and management systems that are used to run the firm's business.

- **products and services**

  This area refers to the professional services which the firm offers to clients as well as any training programmes and professional development schemes it offers to personnel inside the firm.

- **finance**

  This area refers to the firm's assets and liabilities, as well as the system of controls in place to manage resources. Decisions about finance must take into account both the long- and short-term needs of the firm.

- **facilities**

  This area refers to the firm's geographical location, its physical environment (internal and external), as well as its equipment, electronic networks and machinery. The impact of this highly sensitive area is most often ignored when setting objectives. It is vitally important because decisions about leases, capital expense on equipment and office furnishings play an important part in the success of the firm.

- **marketing**

  This area refers to promotion efforts to develop the practice. Plans should include developing contacts, improving client service and assuring service quality so that the firm attracts and maintains its clients.

Practice plans should develop goals for each area even if these goals do not emerge directly from an analysis of the mission statement. For example, when the architectural firm's partners recognize a need for new specialist expertise, they decide to recruit an additional designer. Although this goal *directly* affects the firm's *personnel*, the decision also has an impact on the other four business areas.

Therefore, additional goals should be developed to build upon their having new expertise available for current ongoing projects. As well, decisions should be made for marketing this new service. Finally, financial issues should also be addressed: first, to consider the implications of paying an additional salary and, second, to estimate any hidden costs that new specifications can bring to their projects. Because these costs ultimately affect clients' bills and the firm's year-end profits, these calculations are essential.

There are firms which leave such 'details' until the new person actually arrives to start work. A strategic approach requires the development of complimentary goals so that any new idea, and especially any new person can be better integrated into the firm. Obvious issues should be considered as well as subtle ones. This puts a limit on short-sighted goal setting and plans which enhance one part of the business at the expense of another.

The five external forces

The five business areas refer to the firm's internal activities. The practice is also affected by the outside environment. There are five external forces which influence the success of any organization. These

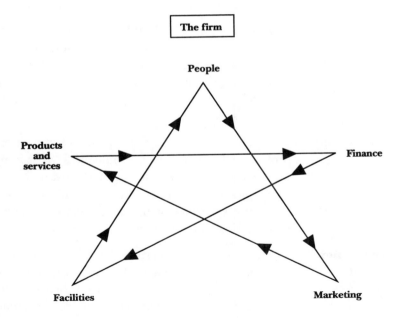

Figure 4.1   The five business areas.

should be fully considered when setting goals for the practice so that the partners develop a strategy for dealing with them. These external forces are:

- government
- social values
- technology
- consumer need
- competition.

Definitions of each are:

- **government** This area refers to political activity of every sort, from legitimate as well as illegitimate authorities. New legislation and terrorist activity can equally affect the firm. Partners should consider past, present and proposed future regulations, insurance, law, procedural codes, taxes and interest rates when setting goals.

- **social values** This area refers to health, education, morals, ethics, and social class issues. Awareness of social thinking is essential when making major decisions about the firm's future. This includes anticipating the impact of peoples' changing attitudes on professional services.

- **technology** This area *seems* to have the least direct impact on professional firms and yet influences *everyone* in business significantly. Issues include awareness of developments which benefit the firm's targeted client market, making use of database management services and innovative computer technology.

- **consumer need** This area refers to the firm's clients: who they are, what they want and where they are located. Goals should be based upon an analysis of their current and potential needs and consider demographic shifts and changes in social values and trends.

- **competition** This area requires partners to be thoroughly aware of initiatives and developments within their profession. Competition provides alternatives to clients. Any planning goals should reinforce the clients' demand for the firm's own services.

While the partners have control over decisions within their firm, they have little or no control over these external forces (see Figure 4.2). The challenge is to study and understand outside events so that the goals of the practice are realistic and truly beneficial to the firm. Firms are in a mutually dependent relationship with their communities. A careful consideration of the five external forces reminds partners of the firm's vulnerability to events outside their direct control.

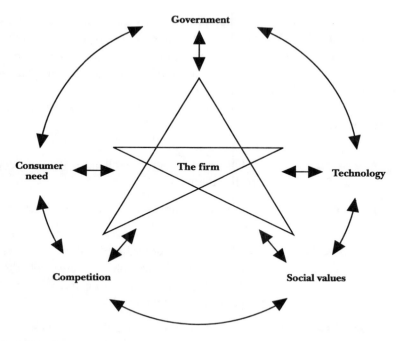

Figure 4.2   The five external forces.

SETTING OBJECTIVES

From vision to mission to goals, planners consider the firm's future in broad and general terms. To ensure that action is taken on these ideas, partners must also set specific objectives for each of their plan's goals. The two following definitions make a distinction between goals and objectives.

A goal is a general and realistic aim for long-term achievement.

An objective describes a specific result to be achieved within a limited and defined period of time. Objectives lead to the accomplishment of goals.

Objectives should be set so that they lead to the achievement of the firm's goals. Each should be checked against other goals and objectives to discover any contradictions or repetitions of effort. This orchestrates practice activity so that objectives harmonize, blend and integrate to serve the needs of the whole firm.

Every objective should include each of the features listed here. Objectives should be:

- **consistent**   They must integrate well into other aspects of the plan.

- **specific**   They must state exactly what end result is desired.

- **measurable**   They must be described so that it is possible to present tangible evidence of their achievement by a named person who is accountable for their results.

- **related to time**   They must have a deadline for their completion.

- **attainable**   They must be realistic in terms of available time, energy and resources.

When objectives are set for each goal, then partners can next decide what actions should be taken. This process is aided if partners ask themselves these questions.

- What actions does this objective require?
- What details must be included?
- How should this be communicated? To whom?
- Who is responsible? To do what? By when?
- How is action to be monitored?

The answers to these questions lead to a detailed list of things to do with the final step in this process actually accomplishing them.

A CAUTIONARY NOTE

Of course, over-planning is to be avoided. A list of objectives in diminishing order of priority for the next twenty years is a mistake. This exercise is valid only if a partner is laid up in bed for an extended period and lacks anything better to do. Plans at their best are sufficiently detailed to encourage activity and yet general enough to allow a flexible response to changing circumstances. Although logically the planning process begins with the partners considering their future, actually it often begins when a partner identifies an important objective. This objective stimulates enough interest among the partners, whether in favour or against, to begin a debate about planning.

Practical and conservative people may argue that it saves time to plan for single objectives in this way. They feel reluctant to discuss vision and the overall purpose of their professional lives. In challenge of this view, case-by-case decision making is effective only when the firm has unlimited resources at its disposal and when the partners have an uncanny ability to agree on all priorities. In a less than ideal world, partners actually save time by considering: first, the general way in which the practice should grow and, second, the specifics of that

Figure 4.3   Planning sequence.

growth. This sequence avoids misunderstandings and disappointment over the long-term outcome of the firm's growth. In summary, a recommended sequence of activity for practice planning is outlined in Figure 4.3.

Again, it should be noted that if the planning process begins with a specific goal or objective, this can serve as a starting point. As soon as contradiction or confusion emerges among the partners, then the debate should be guided to a discussion about vision. Agreement about vision and the purpose of the practice eases decision making about specific goals. When differences of opinion seem slight, this process may seem like using a sledgehammer to crack a nut. Alternatively, decisions which affect the long-term viability of the firm always require a careful consideration of vision.

THE POWER OF MOMENTUM

Having produced a mission statement, the goal setting process best begins with partners agreeing to a financial goal for at least the next five years. Although many professionals dislike considering financial details, they readily offer opinions about the amount of income the firm should produce. Discussion about goals for income at this stage also provides a validity test for the partners' vision.

If there is a gap between how much income the partners want to receive and the work activities they describe in their vision, then either the financial goal or the vision needs further examination. All of the other goals actually hinge on the partners' decision to produce a high or low income. Agreement about financial goals leads to the discussion of goals for the other four business areas. An ambitious decision about income production often demands that partners identify markets, improve services, develop people and modernize facilities.

All of these new goals can then be examined to ensure that they blend together. Coordinated goal setting directly contributes to the firm's success. Figure 4.4 offers a highly rational view of the planning process. The five business areas each provide separate sets of objectives. Each objective ideally enhances all of the others, and should at least avoid contradicting any of them. A cross-check of objectives from each area minimizes repetition and possible wasted effort.

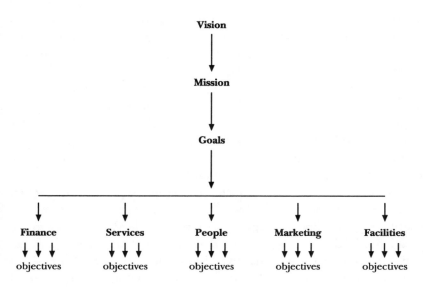

Figure 4.4   A rational view of planning.

Targets

The word target, in terms of planning, can refer to goals in general, but it has assumed a specific meaning when applied to financial goals. In this context, it is the goal that represents the partners' highest financial aspirations for the firm. Three commonly used kinds of financial targets are:

- increased annual earnings for the firm overall
- increased earnings per partner
- increased profit share for partners.

Although analysis of data readily provides figures for all three kinds of targets, it is more effective to select a single kind of target for everyday reference. Not only does this give partners a common point of reference and shared language, but it also has a subtle impact on other issues as well.

For example, the first target listed, 'increased annual earnings', best serves a small firm. When there are only a few partners, they are often aware when their colleagues bring new clients or projects into the firm. Overall increases in practice income are immediately felt and appreciated by everyone. This increases the partners' motivation to develop the firm. This kind of target rallies support when partners fully understand the relationship between the firm's increased income and its effect on their individual profits.

Even so, partners need to be aware that an increase of *gross* income is a deceptive figure. Operating expenses, tax, insurance and other costs must all be deducted before any 'increases' provides a cause for celebration. If it costs more to acquire a new client or to keep a current one than the firm earns from their business, then partners achieve a target but actually gain less than nothing.

The second target listed, 'increased earnings per partner', often leads to healthy competition among partners. Unfortunately, it can also lead to a refusal among partners to share client leads as well as to the creation of independent partner-led empires within a single practice. This kind of target is most useful in firms where partners clearly share common goals, have a similar degree of ambition, and bring goodwill to their partner relationships. Firms which serve a niche market benefit from the use of this target because there are fewer specialist areas represented among the firms' partners and therefore, less likelihood of divisiveness among them.

The third target listed, 'increased profit share', requires partners to watch their overhead expenses as well as their productivity. Because monthly and quarterly figures need some analysis before this target can be readily understood by many professionals, it is a target that is most useful for larger firms with departmental partners or managers. These professionals present brief reports to their colleagues about income and expense on a regular basis (see page 150). As well, there are excellent business software packages available to 'crunch numbers' on a firm's behalf without the cost of an in-house financial analyst.

Inflation

A reference to inflation should be made. Because the figure for inflation fluctuates, it is difficult to compare income amounts from year to year. Therefore, targets should be set in *real terms*, that is, *without* an added amount for inflation. Also, real terms should be used throughout the financial goal-setting process so that current financial figures are also presented in real terms, that is, with inflation removed. This is called 'stripping the figures of inflation'. By subtracting an allowance for inflation, partners can make more accurate comparisons of figures, past, present and future. Once the process of setting a target is complete, then an estimated figure for inflation can be introduced again if this is required.

The following example illustrates the kind of misunderstanding which occurs when inflation is *not removed*. In this case, the annual income generated from one partner's work is £100 000. This partner decides that with extra effort and increased efficiency, the following year's target could be increased to £110 000. This is in *real terms*, that is, inflation is not included in the target.

At the end of the year, the partner is pleased to discover that billings actually rose to £115 000. This certainly looks as if there is a £5000 increase over the targeted amount. In fact, inflation for that year was 5 per cent. To compare actual income to targeted income, the amount for inflation *should be stripped* from the £115 000 figure. A little arithmetic reveals the amount of real income that £115 000 represents:

5 per cent of £115 000 = £5750 inflation

£115 000 billed income − 5 750 inflation=£109 250 = income in *real* terms

The actual amount of earned fees in real terms is £109 250 while the partner's target in real terms is £110 000. This means that the target is short by £750 even though the billings figure of £115 000 initially looked like a cause for celebration.

Forecasts

While targets are based upon the partners' vision and their 'best guess' about the future, forecasts are produced by studying the firm's past and present financial performance. The forecast analyses information about how much income the firm has produced over a period of time. From this, a projection is made about how much income the firm has the potential to earn in the future. This is a similar process to weather forecasting where analysts examine past and present information about the weather to predict its future behaviour.

The forecast is also a measurement of the firm's momentum. The history of the firm's growth gives a strong indication of its growth potential. If the firm continues as it is without change from either outside or inside the practice, then income can be forecasted as a continuation of present rates of growth. As with targets, inflation should be stripped from past and present forecasted figures and should not be included in future income projections. This allows an accurate comparison of all financial figures. Another benefit from producing a financial forecast is the possible discovery of income production trends. This can reveal high and low earning periods or consistently recurring lulls in business activity. An analysis of this information can indicate where and how the practice could be developed.

There is often confusion about the difference between targets and forecasts. The target is linked to the partners' vision for the future. The forecast shows the financial outcome if the firm continues exactly as it is without the influence of any new initiatives or goals. Ideally, the target is higher than the forecast. The difference between them reveals what actions must be taken in order to fill this gap.

A weak financial forecast and a demanding target indicates that partners face challenging years ahead. Their plan of action, therefore, must include goals which change their practice sufficiently so that they can achieve the ambitious target. Occasionally, a review of the gap between a target and a forecast leads partners to alter their targeted figure and therefore set less challenging goals. Achievement of targets benefits a firm only when practice activity is enhanced overall.

The five business areas provide a framework for effective goal setting. For example, increased income could be found by:

- using all facilities to the maximum and improving present efficiency
- offering additional specialist services
- developing new markets
- improving management effectiveness and encouraging staff commitment
- adjusting budgets and tightening financial controls.

Figure 4.5 shows figures for a firm where the partners have decided on a target of £1.5 million turnover within five years' time. Their forecasted income is £1 million. If they are to achieve their target, they need to generate an additional £0.5 million. These partners, then, need a strategy which increases their income by a third. This is ambitious and yet not impossible. It requires concentrated and united effort from all partners and goal setting that is designed specifically to serve income production. An ambitious plan like this only succeeds when everyone involved agrees to the added effort and is convinced that the goals they set are feasible.

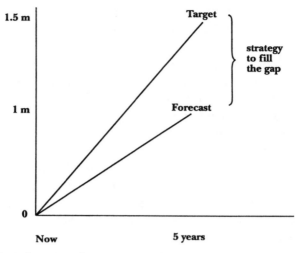

Figure 4.5   Target forecast matrix.

PROBLEM – ANALYSIS – DISCUSSION

Problem

In the mid-1980s, a well respected Scottish architectural firm, won a major contract for designing an airport in Southeast Asia. Subsequently, the ten-partner firm decided to build on their increasing international profile and develop a world-wide client base. Although the Asian project and much of the firm's new business came from the firm's managing partner, the firm's younger partners were in enthusiastic support of his ideas. This younger group of six, four of whom were the children of the firm's founding partners, also strongly believed that the firm's headquarters should be moved to London offices.

Although all ten of the partners discussed the move south in principle, privately the firm's elder partners had strong reservations. They withheld their comments because they did not wish to dampen their younger colleagues' enthusiasm and also believed that they would gradually see the negative aspects of the idea. Following their presentation of the London move idea, the six younger partners assumed they had tacit consent to develop their plans. They formed a planning task force just as the managing partner left for Asia and a short sabbatical away from the firm.

Exploring the London move took considerable time as the young partners had to schedule numerous meetings in London. Unfortunately, some clients' deadlines were missed and a few ongoing projects were gradually falling behind schedule as a result. They rationalized these lapses because they believed that they were acting for the firm's long-term benefit, and after all, they owned an equal share of equity in the firm with their senior colleagues.

Eight months after the meeting to discuss the move, the young partners finally chose a property and actually scheduled a meeting to sign a lease. This coincided with the return of the managing partner from sabbatical, as well as the completion of a major project in the Mediterranean area, which had been headed by the firm's financial partner. At the first full partners' meeting in eight months, the six younger members announced their results and presented their plans for the London venture in detail.

For the first time, the young partners learned that the 'old guard' had never intended moving south. Furthermore, these partners expressed considerable anger about the time 'these puppies' had spent on the move and their poor fee performance as a result. The junior partners were accused of 'wasting valuable practice time' and 'not earning their keep for almost a year'. The discussion became very heated indeed when the son of the managing partner disclosed how much practice money had actually been spent in pursuit of this new venture.

Analysis

1   In what ways would a discussion of vision benefit these ten partners?

2   What is the likely impact of their collective behaviour upon the firm's staff and non-partners?

3   What are the goals of the elder partners in terms of the five business areas?

4   What are the goals of the younger partners in terms of these areas?

5   How do these differences contribute to their contradictory objectives?

Discussion

This problem shows two groups reaching a point of confrontation because they hold very different ideas about their firm's future based on different expectations and understanding. Although the elder partners are able to see that they are partly to blame for not giving their colleagues more direction and guidance, they also believe that their colleagues' behaviour has been completely irresponsible. The younger partners do realize that they should have consulted their older colleagues, but also feel tricked and deceived by them.

Although the elder partners withheld their reservations about the London move because they wished to encourage their colleagues' enthusiasm, they also denied them the benefit of their experience. Their explosion of anger is in complete contradiction to the consent that they implied by their former silence and the lack of any supervision of the young partners' activities during an eight-month period. Withholding their opinion from their partners, even with benign intentions, has damaged their professional relationships and, therefore, the practice as a whole.

Lack of clarity among the partners is likely to cause considerable unease and disquiet throughout the whole firm. Certainly, the firm's staff and associates have realized that there are two diametrically opposed factions developing within the firm. When a rumour circulates about a headquarter's move and there is no forum for staff to discover its accuracy, then a highly charged atmosphere develops. In this case, staff are caused unnecessary stress which, in turn, affects their motivation and commitment to the firm.

The elder partners' goals include encouraging their colleagues' enthusiasm but also expecting them to do an equal share of the work. While they seek new markets, they intend to keep their local business as well. The partners' obvious success leads them to take their financial goals for granted. It is an area which they have always managed well, at least until the emergence of the current partnership problems.

The younger partners also want to develop new markets and yet equate this growth with a move to a new location. Their lack of management experience leads them to rationalize their poor productivity as an investment in the future. If it were an investment, they would either have new business to show for their effort or, at least, an analysis of what impeded this. Like their older colleagues, they seem to take financial goals for granted. In their case, this is more dangerous because they have never managed a budget or been responsible for paying the firm's bills.

These differences in goals lead directly to major misunderstanding. The main cause of this situation is the partners' assumption that they share a common vision for the firm's future. A discussion that addressed each partners' ambitions and wishes for the future would reveal this discrepancy in goals. Only when they reach an agreement about vision, mission and goals will they be able to develop common objectives.

SUMMARY

This chapter emphasizes the importance of partners agreeing to a vision for the future. This agreement provides the basis for developing a mission statement for the practice. It is suggested that practice goals should be developed from an analysis of the firm's mission. When goals are linked to the partners' ambitions, then any plans to achieve these goals are readily implemented. A distinction is made between goals and objectives, and criteria are provided for setting clear objectives. Both goals and objectives, should refer to the five internal business areas and five external forces. Finally, it is recommended that the planning process is best served when financial targets are considered first and then used as an 'acid test' for other planning goals.

5

Decision making

THE BENEFIT OF HINDSIGHT

With hindsight, disastrous decisions always seem avoidable and their outcomes obvious, so much so that their originators appear consciously to have chosen catastrophe. The following three examples provide powerful illustrations of this.

Example 1

A construction project runs into unforeseen difficulties so that its overrun costs are £5 million per week. The project leader immediately informs his employer, a firm of construction engineers, on learning the scale of their potential loss. He firmly believes that construction cannot be completed and says so.

The client has been told and yet fears that the news of the project's failure will cause the banks to call in their loans. Therefore, the client refuses to stop the project even as costs escalate. The firm of construction engineers 'decides' to carry on by choosing not to stop the project themselves.

Example 2

In the 1960s, an architectural firm develops plans for a 40-storey, mirror-sided skyscraper and promotes this as the first ever computer-designed building. The partners explain that human input on design has been kept to a minimum. Meteorologists and construction engineers warn the developers against using a newly designed glass for that location and that kind of structure. Even so, building goes ahead as planned.

On the first occasion of a gale-force wind, the sheets of glass panelling shake loose from their sidings, shatter and fall to the streets below. Luckily no one is hurt. After urgent meetings, an emergency solution substitutes wood panels for the glass until a new window material is available.

Example 3

A group of medical doctors gain government funding for a famine relief project. In spite of warnings from representatives of an international health organization, they entrust distribution to local stewardship with criminal associations. Later, the doctors discover that there is massive misappropriation of funds, medicine and supplies.

Lacking management skills, their attempts to correct the situation drive the few honest brokers away and encourage the dishonest ones to use even more covert means of theft. The doctors decide to carry on even though they realize that only 20 per cent of donations reach the people in need. They fear that adverse publicity will dry up funding entirely and they are committed to their project.

In all three of these examples, the decision makers received clear warnings of potential disaster. In fact:

Example 1: The construction engineers should have stopped the project before more unrecoverable costs were incurred for their own firm.

Example 2: The architects should have integrated advice based upon human experience with their computer system's rudimentary programmes.

Example 3: The doctors should have stopped distribution of supplies and thoroughly reorganized their system.

They all chose to go ahead because, at the time, this seemed the best choice available. These examples are based on actual events and, historically, the projects failed completely bringing financial ruin to the first, ridicule to the second, and disgrace to the third. These examples are somewhat more dramatic than most firms' everyday decision-making situations, and yet there are similarities. They each highlight the kinds of dilemmas which face professionals on a regular basis: when to say 'stop', when to change direction, and when to reorganize completely.

Decision makers not only need *techniques* for making decisions, they also need to recognize the *kind of thinking* which consistently contributes to effective decision making and the *kind of organization* which makes wise decision making a standard practice. This chapter addresses all three of these issues.

THEORY AND PRACTICE

Although clients seek advice, not decisions from a professional practice, that advice is based upon the professional's expert opinion about the client's wisest course of action. In this sense, professionals are extremely adept decision makers. While individual personalities determine the degree of caution, creativity or perception they bring to their advice, all successful professionals know how to process information, accept formidable responsibility and recommend action with confidence. This is the service for which clients pay a fee.

Decision making about technical matters is an assumed area of expertise. For many practice leaders, it is natural and relatively easy to apply this skill to business decisions as well. For others, it is more difficult. Although the mental discipline is the same, these professionals bring less interest to business matters and practice management than to the practice of their profession. The sobering examples at the beginning of this chapter illustrate the impact which business decisions have on a professional firm and argue the importance of practice-wide decision-making skills.

It is beneficial to examine how experts actually formulate professional advice. This process begins even as they listen to their clients describing a problem. The nature of their profession determines relevance so that a solicitor, an accountant and a construction engineer each listens to a single client's problem and highlights different issues as the essentials of the case.

Professional training provides the discipline for organizing and analysing information as well as the technical knowledge for interpreting what is heard. This efficient and selective listening forms the basis for the professionals' subsequent advice. Next, they explore the salient issues more deeply toward formulating a course of action. Although this may result in their presenting the client with several options, their professional role requires considering, deciding and then suggesting which choice is wisest and serves their client best.

The process of formulating professional advice can be summarized in the following way:

- maintaining a professional point of view
- listening to the client and gathering information
- analysing issues to define essential points
- proposing action in line with best practice.

The decision-making process for business management has much in common with the process of offering professional advice. These four steps can equally apply to making decisions with partners for the practice. The points of difference between the two decision-making requirements are emphasized in italics below:

- maintaining a *business* point of view
- listening to *colleagues* and gathering information
- analysing issues to define essential points
- *discussing issues with colleagues* and proposing action.

There is an inherent risk in presenting an important function like decision making as a four-step process. This simplification seemingly endorses a superficial response to an important topic. Management decision making is complex and requires as much concentration as does professional consultation. The purpose here is to highlight the similarities between providing expert advice to clients and giving appropriate attention to management for the firm. It emphasizes the importance of considering business affairs with the same gravity that is readily given to client issues.

While the *process* of decision making can be systematized into four steps as it is here, the *exercise* of that process is far more challenging and varies from firm to firm. Much available management advice ignores the realities facing decision makers, including lack of information, an inability to articulate, covert influences, stupidity and biased points of view. These are facts of life in any business. As well, this advice leaves unconsidered the difficulties of applying suggested methods to highly pressurized situations.

As an antidote to human frailty, as well as a preparation for crisis situations, a firm's internal organization and decision-making process can be organized so that these ensure viable business decisions. As well, every firm needs a forum for its members to discuss important decisions. This stimulates open debate and formalizes its occurrence. The way a firm is organized, the presence of a consistent and stable system of management and regular discussion among the partners all contribute to successful decision making.

Those partners who, for whatever reason, abdicate their decision making responsibility lose the opportunity to influence the firm's future direction. By default, their peers or even random circumstances decide the firm's future although these partners continue to be fiscally and legally responsible for its decisions.

CASE STUDY: CHANTREY VELLACOTT CHARTERED ACCOUNTANTS

The purpose of this case study is to illustrate the professional firm's need for a clearly defined decision-making policy. The Managing Partner involved describes his firm's organizational structure and its procedures for decision making.

The firm of Chantrey Vellacott Chartered Accountants has 38 partners with headquarters in London and six branch offices. It is managed by a team of three which includes the Managing, Financial and Development Partners. John Roberts, the firm's Managing Partner, suggests that this number provides a balanced representation of the partnership and yet is small enough to respond quickly to important issues. He believes that the team's decision-making capability is a vital management function.

In his words, 'The most critical feature for a professional firm is its decision making. Because a partnership is made up of equals, there has to be a structure which enables decisions to be made. Otherwise, you end up with a number of different perspectives and angles and no decision at all. After a few years of this, you may find yourself out of the game.'

'A small management team' never means one person in John's view. 'One person as a practice decision maker can't reflect the partners' opinions. It is true that some partners may feel complacent when things are going well because financial rewards compensate for a lack of participation, but some others can never get satisfaction from the partnership unless they feel enfranchised. As a long-term solution, an autocratic leader in a partnership doesn't work.

'A partnership of ten could probably meet up and make a decision as long as they have a good chairman. From 10 to about 20 partners, the team should have at least two part-time decision makers to manage the firm. From 20 to possibly 50 partners, there should be a small team of full-time managers with high-level management support from non-partners. These are just estimates of course.'

There comes a point in a partnership when the size of the firm undermines its ability to function as a true partnership. Instead, it gradually develops into a corporate entity. John says, 'Partners who join this kind of firm don't expect to play a role in practice management. In the very large firms, partners have line responsibility for their departmental operations. They are called partners and take profit shares, but in terms of decision making and planning strategy for the partnership's future, they play very little role. A corporate style of decision making is an effective one for a large-sized firm. In smaller firms, partners are actively involved in planning and participate in major decisions. They like this and want to remain in it.

'At Chantrey Vellacott, we have a body of partners who historically have been involved in the running of the business. Because the firm has grown, they are now less involved, but participate in formal monthly partnership briefings, and we hold twice yearly full partnership meetings. Also, the management team is not cocooned away, we talk to our fellow partners on a day to day basis.'

The firm also has other forums for discussion and debate. It is organized into business units, each with a managing partner, a finance partner and a development partner. This team mirrors the functions of the firm's three-person management team and thereby creates functional links across all departmental divisions. For example, the firm's development partner maintains regular contact with all of the departmental development partners. This gives the firm the benefits of specialized service through its departmental structure. It also creates a network across the departments which allows the firm's management team to maintain contact with their partners and monitor the firm's activities effectively.

Referring to alternative decision-making styles, John says, 'I recently visited a legal firm which operates in teams on a matrix model [see page 125]. Each team is responsible to go out and pull in business. They are so focused on the top line [generating income] they haven't taken into account the bottom line [managing costs to produce profit]. There is no purpose in getting business if it costs more to pull in and undertake than the firm actually recovers through the work. There are too many professional firms which don't even keep time records. A firm needs sufficient and consistent financial information on which to base its management decisions.'

In John's view, a decision is a good one if it resolves a problem or allows the firm to gain an opportunity. It has to be capable of implementation, to assist in achieving the firm's objectives and to satisfy the partnership's wishes. A poor decision is one which puts the firm at risk, gives the competition an advantage or to which most of the partners cannot agree.

John also believes that the firm's business units should make as many decisions as possible. This is in part because it involves people in the business. As well, he adds, 'The top team needs to concentrate on the bigger issues and those which involve more than one unit. Each business unit has a minuted monthly meeting with an agenda which we [the management team] help to set. As decisions are made, we learn about them. Any decision with a significant financial implication, we see very quickly. Generally, the partners come and talk to us about the decision before it is made.

'When there is a problem, we try to get the people involved to resolve it themselves. If necessary, the management team acts as a facilitator but avoids making the final decision on their behalf. Ideally, they sort out their problems with help, then the next time around they can deal with it entirely themselves. I would like both partners and firm employees to be more empowered to recognize real problems and take decisions to provide solutions for themselves. To get a good growth rate and profitability, any firm must recognize the problems and opportunities which exist and resolve or capitalize on them.' This requires good decision making.

PRACTICE ORGANIZATION

The way in which a practice is organized enhances or undermines its decision-making ability. Partners improve management effectiveness through a regular review of the way in which they run the firm and a re-examination of the thinking behind their management system. This in-house evaluation potentially reveals outmoded leadership styles, unnecessary paperwork, inefficiency or ineffective communication within the firm.

John Roberts suggests that the number of partners should influence the firm's decision-making system. At Chantrey Vellacott, a small team represents the other partners' business and professional interests and is accountable to them through reports and regular meetings. Even so, in clearly defined areas, this team has authority to act on behalf of the firm without referral to the body of partners. A system such as this can work only when partners are willing to delegate responsibility to a few colleagues so that the firm is managed using a limited form of hierarchy. Although this hierarchy is one that they create themselves, many partners in professional firms resist handing over management of business affairs to others. This often directly contradicts their resistance to managing business matters themselves.

Each firm has its own unique management system and its long-term success depends upon how well it reflects the wishes of the collected partners. The form this system takes is very often a mixture of two organizational models: the hierarchy and the matrix. The following sections present a brief history of the development of these models. The purpose of this is to encourage an analysis of their relevance to an individual professional practice. Background information such as this often reveals hidden aspects of old ideas so that new and specialized applications can be discovered.

A third model for practice organization, network management, is also proposed. This deliberately blends features of both matrix and hierarchy to suggest a model suited to professional firms. Analysis 5 (see page 131) encourages practice leaders to evaluate their present organization and define the model they currently use to organize their firm.

Management by hierarchy

Background

The word 'hierarchy' is based on two Greek words, '*hieros*' meaning sacred, and '*archein*', meaning rule. In ancient civilizations, those who ruled drew their authority from a sacred or religious source. Their closeness to the gods was their source of precedence over other citizens and this entitled them to be designated leaders. Social standing within society was based upon an individual's relationship with the significant few who were the leaders.

Although the religious connotation is removed from the role of leader in contemporary society, some elements of this association remain. The very concept of 'leader' is based upon the idea that a single person or set of persons can be authorized to act on behalf of others. The religious source for this authority has disappeared, but the distinction between leaders and followers remains.

In fact, this notion is so deeply ingrained in human society that it is simply assumed as natural that leaders and followers emerge within any collection of people. Regardless of economic system, racial origin or technological advance, hierarchy is the most common model for organizations across the world, whether government, religious, military, commercial or professional. There are exceptions, but these are by far a minority.

Of course, anthropologists address this issue in depth, and, admittedly, hierarchy *as a social phenomenon* is an unusual subject for inclusion in a book on management methods. Even so, this aspect of hierarchy is relevant here because it highlights the historical precedent for the widespread use of grades for organizing people. It also serves as a reminder that people readily accept being grouped into top and bottom positions *even when they are not required to do so*. This is very interesting when considering the relevance of hierarchy for organizing the members of a professional firm.

Hierarchy, for business, is beneficial whenever work must be organized so that tasks are divided into segments or subtasks. The development of division of labour in manufacturing, historically marks the need for the highly formalized use of hierarchy within business organizations. Mass production requires many people to complete subtasks instead of a single person to complete a single task.

When several individuals work together to complete segments of a single task, then this increases the need for managers to coordinate their work effort and monitor overall completion of tasks. These coordinators are always fewer in number and have greater authority than those who complete the subtasks. This basic hierarchical model is illustrated in Figure 5.1.

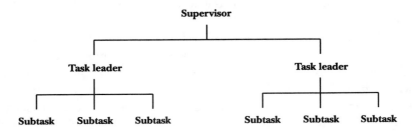

Figure 5.1   Division of labour.

Those at the top of the hierarchy divide the tasks, appoint the task completers, supervise their work and encourage cooperative effort among all of the task completers. The benefits of division of tasks and labour are significant. These include increased productivity, uniform quality and control of volume and costs. With these benefits, though, comes the risk of increased interdependence among all of the segmented tasks. In an organization where each individual completes each product independently, one individual's failure impacts only a single item. When many individuals complete parts of a product together, a single individual impacts all of the units produced. The obvious advantage of labour division must be weighed against the need for supervision, communication and coordination of effort.

Hierarchy as a model is far less useful when there is little need to divide tasks, and there is only minor distinction of skill and function among those completing the tasks. To determine the need for labour division and, by inference, the need for a formalized hierarchy, an audit of tasks and subtasks should be conducted. The issues to be examined include:

- What are the firms' essential tasks?
- Can or should these tasks be divided?
- How should they be divided?
- What kind of supervision is needed?

Answers to these questions lead to decisions about the usefulness of hierarchical management for *specific tasks* or *for a whole firm*. As well, this evaluation allows discovery of the form which the hierarchy should take.

A hierarchy can produce a 'tall and thin' organization, with many management levels each supervising two or three individuals, or to a 'flat' organization, with a few management levels supervising as many as 100 individuals (see Figure 5.2). Whatever the shape, a hierarchical system requires everyone to know the nature of their responsibilities and to whom they report within the organization's chain of command.

The tall and thin organization

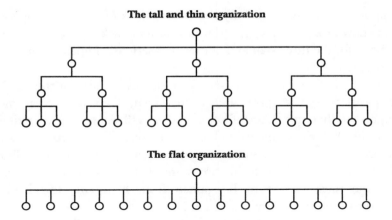

The flat organization

Figure 5.2   Two forms of hierarchy.

Application

This background information leads to a discussion of the hierarchical model's relevance to the professional organization. In a partnership, there are usually several partners who own the firm and have equal authority. This multi-leader situation introduces ambiguity into the chain of command and potentially creates confusion among non-partners and staff. Even if there is just one elected senior or managing partner, all of the partners remain equal-level leaders of the firm because they are its owners.

This situation is illustrated in Figure 5.3. It shows an example of six partners with three support staff. Although this figure looks upside down, it is a situation of hierarchy because the partners own the firm and their support staff do not. As well, there is division of labour so that the staff contribute segments of clerical support to the firm. What this situation requires is a clear chain of command so that the three

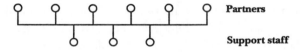

Partners

Support staff

Figure 5.3   Simplified professional hierarchy.

support staff understand fully the expectations of their six employers and know to whom they report. If this clarity is lacking, life is extremely difficult for the three staff and efficiency is seriously impaired for the six partners.

If a level of associates or junior professionals is added or the number of partners and support staff is increased, then it is even more important that the chain of command is well defined. This requires that there is clear understanding of responsibilities throughout the organization, that channels of communication are established throughout all levels of the hierarchy and that all tasks are well defined. For the most benefit to be gained from hierarchy, this kind of coordination is necessary.

There are two other potential problems. The first of these concerns motivation. Completion of subtasks is most suited to junior levels within a professional firm. As these juniors become more skilled, it is possible to rotate subtasks so that they all gradually become skilled at the completion of a whole task. When this training cycle is complete, these skilled junior professionals have no further opportunity to progress.

This is particularly true in a firm with rigidly defined boundaries between specialisms. Ideally, trained juniors from one division transfer to another and begin the process again by learning each subtask in turn until they gain full proficiency. In many firms, this kind of job rotation is discouraged. The juniors 'belong' to a division and must accept that a rise in the firm means waiting for promotion opportunities within that division. Transfer is difficult because the firm has invested heavily in their skill development for one specialist area.

Within industry, a ceiling on advancement is more readily accepted, although grudgingly, and the transfer from one company area to another is often an available option. Alternatively, ambitious professionals who have invested years of their lives in education and training, find that such limitation to career progress is very difficult to accept. When career prospects look dim, the best of them look outside the firm for new challenges. The others, whether less ambitious or talented, remain where they are as long as the firm allows them to do so.

Another potential problem for hierarchy within a professional firm concerns the motivation of those who are at the top of the practice. When they assign their actual client work to junior firm members or associates as a series of subtasks, these partners assume roles as educators, quality inspectors and public relations figures. Those professionals who prefer the actual practice of their profession can feel less inspired when required to supervise the delivery of client service by other less experienced practice members.

The development of a complex hierarchy can gradually emerge as partners decide to train associates and juniors to complete segments of work which they originally completed themselves. It is a healthy exercise for partners to assess their satisfaction with their present style of work. If they find that they are increasingly doing supervisory work which they never intended to take on, this should be discussed among the partners and a resolution found.

Matrix management

Background

The use of a matrix to organize working teams became formalized as a model for business during the 1960s. Although the idea has historic roots as ancient as those of hierarchy, its popularity in the twentieth century is most likely linked to the development of the aerospace industry in the United States. Although no single entrepreneur or academic lays claim to this application, Donald Kingdon, in his book *Matrix Organizations*, suggests that its origins emerge from contract bids for research projects. In order to qualify for US government contracts, companies in the 1960s had to submit charts describing how the proposed project would be organized and how the project's personnel related to top management.

Because these firms traditionally are organized according to functions, such as engineering, finance, personnel or design, the proposal writers presented the required bid information in the form of a matrix. The horizontal axis showed the functional groups and the vertical axis presented the project groups. This format allowed a client to see immediately the specialist area of the staff who were engaged in

	Engineering	Research	Finance	Administration	Production
Project A	X	X			X
Project B	X	X	X	X	
Project C		X X		X	X

Figure 5.4   Project management matrix.

a given project. An example of a project management matrix is presented in Figure 5.4.

This example presents three projects. Each engages individuals from different functional areas of the firm. The matrix gives a client or the firm's management an instant overview of the project team's composition with reference to members' functional backgrounds.

The matrix model offers further detail when the individuals involved in the project are named on the vertical axis as shown in Figures 5.5. Because a project includes the efforts of several departments, the matrix enables clients to deal directly with the designated project leader and avoid having to contact several different department heads along a chain of command. Use of the matrix model allows responsibility to be assigned to a specific person who then represents the project to the rest of the company as well as to clients. As well, this model highlights the areas of specialism or expertise possessed by team members.

The purest form of matrix management is found in an equi-status team of specialists drawn together for a specific project. The team and its individual members have an open-ended relationship with the other teams of specialists within the same firm. As projects arise, these specialists join the project teams either by recruitment or request. With

	Engineering	Research	Finance	Administration	Production
Project leader	X				
Member A		X			
Member B					X

Figure 5.5 Matrix for project A.

matrix management, the coordination and control of resources becomes crucial because team formation and dissolution is so fluid. The firm's viability depends upon maintaining a careful balance of finance, human resources and facilities.

There is further management challenge because the use of a matrix system dilutes the authority of an organization's top or central management. Although the organization as a whole continues to be led by its senior managers, these leaders defer technical decisions to the project teams. As a result, considerable decision-making authority is given to the project team experts. Because the authority of central management is weakened, when problems do occur within projects, individual members must resolve these themselves. The matrix model is flexible enough to support such concentrated problem-solving among experts, but project team members require excellent communication skills and an ability to resolve conflicts as they arise. This is easier said than done.

The matrix model enjoyed considerable popularity during the 1970s with management theorists promoting it as *the means* for empowering and motivating employees. Critics of the hierarchical model suggested that use of a matrix system of management is more adaptable, responsive to changing environmental requirements and also more democratic.

Unfortunately, it has its drawbacks. Jay Galbraith, in his book, *Organization Structure*, suggests that management by matrix is the most difficult and expensive system to employ within large organizations with high task interdependence, changing consumer requirements and a need to integrate large amounts of information from internal and external sources. Greater complexity increases the need to process information. The matrix model does not lend itself to easing the difficulties of information overload.

Application

Despite its difficulties, the matrix system has much to offer professional firms. Jay Galbraith's reservations primarily address the escalating requirements of organizations which must manage enormous amounts of information. The professional firm is less subject to this stress because services are based upon personal know-how rather than technology, volume production and distribution of goods.

Also, a requirement for the successful use of matrix management is the development of clearly defined areas of specialism. Professionals are usually grouped into specialist areas already. For example, a project team within an accounting firm can include a tax specialist, an auditor and a commercial development adviser. This team collaborates so that the client experiences a 'seamless' service, unaware that different experts contribute advice. The project team for multi-service provision is a beneficial choice for advising a client with extensive service needs.

One difficulty cited for matrix management is the challenge of reporting to two bosses. The term 'boss' refers both to the project leader and the department heads to whom individual project team members must report. In professional firms, there are as many bosses as there are partners. The need for thorough and continual communication is obvious and, therefore, is more likely to be fully addressed. The communication system which a professional firm develops to manage its ongoing business is likely to be very effective when applied to the demands of matrix management.

The matrix system is a highly flexible one and provides a forum for shared expertise to the advantage of the client. As well, professional practice lends itself to the formation of teams. It is also an ideal way to apportion the time of junior firm members so that they are trained in a variety of specialist areas. This is healthier than limiting their work to the completion of the subtasks of one specialist area.

Network management

This system blends features of hierarchy with those of a matrix. Such a mixture is beneficial to professional firms because it integrates the flexibility of a matrix with the stability of hierarchy. In the Chantrey Vellacott case study, John Roberts describes the firm's management team and its relationship to the rest of the partners. This approach includes *features of hierarchy* because the team is authorized to make certain decisions on the partners' behalf. They are also responsible for maintaining tight financial controls and so they are arguably in 'top' positions within the firm. The firm's management system also includes *features of the matrix model*. In this case, the project team consists of the members of this management group. Although each partner is responsible for a specific management area, they are also a defined team with the project of practice management. A matrix which would illustrate this situation is presented as Figure 5.6.

	Administration	Finance	Marketing
Managing Partner	X		
Finance Partner		X	
Marketing Partner			X

Figure 5.6   Project team: practice management.

	Top team	Dept 1	Dept 2	Dept 3
Finance Partner	X			
Finance Representative		X		
Finance Representative			X	
Finance Representative				X

Figure 5.7   Project team: finance network.

John Roberts also describes how to expand upon a matrix model in the Chantrey Vellacott case study. For example, each of the firm's departments has a unit representative, a finance representative and a marketing representative. These representatives together form three project teams which meet regularly with the three members of the firm's top team. During these sessions, they discuss issues related to the three project areas of finance, marketing and the administration of the practice. If this were presented as a matrix, it would be presented as Figure 5.7. In this example, the network which is composed of all practice members with responsibility for *finance* meets together regularly.

Blending the advantages of hierarchy with those of matrix management provides a balanced structure for professional firms. It includes a 'chain of command' so that communication, quality supervision, cost control and other essential issues are given proper attention by leaders in clearly defined roles. It also allows a flexible response to needs for change because project teams can readily be formed to focus on specific issues as they arise. A strong network of contacts is also created throughout the firm based upon cross-functional team relationships. Analysis 5 offers questions for analysis of the firm's current organizational system.

Analysis 5

1 Every organization has a structure even if it is not obvious. Please sketch out an organizational chart for your practice distinguishing each level of the organization in terms of ownership, expertise, professional and support staff.

2 Can you identify the chain of command at a glance?

3 Determine where there is a lack of clarity in roles or functions.

4 Do all juniors, associates and staff know to whom they report and where they 'fit' into the organization?

5 Do all juniors, associates and staff know whom to contact to offer good ideas, gain information or make complaints?

6 Where in the firm are examples of matrix management or project teams?

7 How is communication managed between project teams and the firm's central management? Between the departments and the firm's central management?

8 Areas which lack clarity provide partners with issues for discussion and decision making.

RUNNING THE BUSINESS

Almost 100 years ago, the economist Vilfredo Pareto, suggested that, within society at large, 20 per cent of the people produce 80 per cent of the results. This is often referred to as the '20 to 80 ratio'. Some business leaders respond literally to this theory and decide which 20 per cent of their workforce is crucial to their business and which 80 per cent is not. They then set about getting rid of the identified 80 per cent. Unfortunately, this solution oversimplifies to absurdity the meaning of Pareto's 20 to 80 ratio.

Identifying the high producers within a firm is always easy. It is much more difficult to determine exactly how the rest of the firm contributes to this production. For example, if the firm's 'high flyers' were to work alone, they would be far less productive. To apply the 20 to 80 ratio, 20 per cent of their effort would go into producing 80 per cent of their results. Even though they are likely to continue to produce high-quality work, their efficiency decreases because they assume numerous support tasks themselves. The question is, which of their activities are wasted effort and which contribute directly to productivity.

Increased efficiency and productivity are desirable and possible goals and yet their achievement requires deeper thinking than simply cutting away activities, projects or people which are most obviously expensive to the firm or seemingly offer only a minor contribution. Because the firm as a whole is a system of interrelated parts, it is rather like a house made of playing cards with each level and individual member resting upon all of the others. Before deciding to alter any part, careful consideration should be given to the impact of a single change upon the rest of the structure.

Decisions about complex issues which promise quick and easy solutions should always be suspect. Care, balance, tact and time are needed most when issues concern the viability and success of the firm. Effective decision making depends upon integrating new choices and directions so that they blend into the current organizational system and achieve its long-term goals. This requires checking how a decision affects all of the work areas and each of the processes which comprise the management of the firm.

Work in process

By definition, *a management process is a set of tasks and procedures which contribute to the completion of the firm's business.* Some examples of business processes are mail delivery, record storage, billing and purchasing, among others. As well, each professional service offered by the firm includes numerous tasks for the completion of this technical work. Each *set of tasks* is a process, as are the actions taken to maintain client contact and to develop new business. For example, the valuation department of a firm of chartered surveyors has a process for billing clients. This billing process overlaps that used by all of the other departments within the firm. If the valuation partner decides to change client billing, this not only has an impact on the firm as a whole, but also creates much unnecessary confusion.

Even a technical change to the provision of a specific service can have a knock-on effect throughout the firm. Alterations should be examined in terms of how they impact other specialist services or the provision of administrative support. When practice leaders identify key practice processes in need of improvement, such as client billing, it is best if this leads to discussion throughout the organization about the present system's degree of effectiveness and the features which need alteration. This step allows coordinated effort and avoids different departments developing different processes to achieve similar tasks. Improvement made to client billing in the valuation department should be planned so that it coincides with change across all of the other departments. This creates greater efficiency and a more consistent and unified service for the client.

This approach requires partners and staff to think about the firm and their work in a new way. It means that decision making about change within the firm should be linked to an assessment of how each choice affects the overall running of the practice. This offers advance preparation for potential disruption and allows plans to be made which anticipate possible implementation problems.

When decisions are made without considering their effects on the firm as a whole, difficulties invariably arise. The following example illustrates this. The top management of an international accounting firm decided to set standard times for the shift schedules of all non-professional staff in the London office. This was in response to abuses they discovered with flexi-time scheduling. Unexpectedly, an indirect result of this decision was a daily pile-up of morning post in the mail room waiting to be logged and sorted.

The mail room supervisor was powerless to mobilize additional staff or begin the work day at an earlier time because the firm's London managers refused to discuss exceptions and special cases, even after the supervisor explained the mail room's specific needs. Only after irate partners delegated staff members to investigate the source of late mail delivery, could action be taken to correct this situation.

This example illustrates the need to consider the firm as a whole system when making decisions. Genuine improvements address the root cause of problems and usually enhance several processes at once. In this example, a decision was made to address the single process of scheduling. Practice leaders needed also to consider what impact a decision about this single process would have upon the firm as a whole. In fact, the mail delivery process was only one of the many problems created by this decision. Even obvious and common-sense decisions to change a process require careful consideration because each process is linked to all of the others. Effective decision making depends upon recognizing and working with this.

Improving a process

Responsibility for improving a company process rests with the firm's partners and higher level management. Junior staff, such as mail delivery clerks or their supervisors are powerless to correct a process error even if they are in a position to identify it as such. Too often, junior members of a firm can seem to be avoiding responsibility when they explain that a process-related problem is not their fault. A process approach requires looking into the tasks which comprise each process as well as identifying how a change to the process affects other practice areas. The goal is to discover the real cause of a problem and resolve this.

'If it ain't broke, don't fix it.' This traditional American proverb suggests that there is a lack of wisdom in tinkering with successful activities, and yet in this instance, the purpose of anticipating trouble is to avoid allowing problems to develop later. Examining the firm's processes often brings to light surprising information. A solution aimed at ridding the firm of a problem may do so, but at the expense of developing a different problem in another part of the firm, as in the mail room example.

When partners make a decision to improve the firm's management, they should ask if their decisions will remedy weakness across all related areas within the practice or, at least, avoid aggravating any current problem situations. This is challenging because the view from the top of the practice is wide and encompassing rather than detailed and distinct. Problems often appear at points within an organization far removed from their origins, and it is therefore difficult to trace their source.

In one example, the management team of a mid-sized firm decided to introduce a new time-recording system in order to improve their process for billing clients. This was in response to long-standing complaints from clients who wanted more detailed billing information. The partners researched the problem and decided to adopt a sophisticated software package requiring departmental secretaries to key in the time totals for monthly bills. This information would then be fed automatically to the accounts department and, therefore, remove the pressure created by their having to enter all of the billing information at the end of each month.

Because the partners recognized the need to train the staff to use the software, they thoroughly planned for this aspect of the process, as well as for equipment purchase and the efficient exchanges of information between the secretarial and accounts department staff. The one area which they overlooked addressed the need for professional firm members, at the first stage of this new process, to log their client time accurately on time sheets. In fact, if truth were told, it was the firm's 40 partners' consistent unwillingness to complete time sheets correctly and on schedule that was the major cause of billing difficulties for the accounts department.

Although the billing problem seemed to be caused by an overloaded accounts staff who seemed unable to present adequate information to the client, this was just a symptom. At least one member of the management team fully recognized this and his endorsement of the software solution was based on a secret hope that it would woo his colleagues into cooperation. Unfortunately, it did not.

Process improvement then includes these two main points:

- identify all the tasks and activities needed to complete the process
- assess how decisions concerning one process impact the rest of the firm.

In the example of time recording, the partners' completion of the time sheets was one task which the planners overlooked. As a result, their software solution could not address this essential issue. Even so, this team was very successful in identifying how billing improvement would impact the rest of the firm. They planned for training, purchasing and communication in order to keep disruption to a minimum.

This initial clarity ultimately served their improvement plan because it highlighted the lack of cooperation among the professional members of the firm. With a highly efficient new system in place, the management team could put additional pressure on their colleagues who could no longer blame other staff for their own shortcomings for billing problems.

To return to Pareto's 20 to 80 ratio, a process approach examines how tasks and procedures relate to each other. When decisions need to be made to improve efficiency, recognizing how the 80 per cent contributes to the 20 per cent helps avoid altering features of the firm which are critical to its success or, at least its well-being.

Analysis 6

This analysis focuses on how to use process improvement for decision making.

1   Think of an example of a current problem within the firm. Summarize this in two or three sentences.

2   What process is affected by this problem?

3   List all of the tasks and activities required to complete this process.

4   How does completion of these tasks and activities affect the rest of the firm?

5   List all the other processes affected by the tasks and activities associated with the targeted process.

6   Assess the proposed decision in terms of its affect on these processes.

CLEAR AGREEMENT, POLICIES AND PROCEDURES

The partnership agreement

The process of decision making is made easier when partners have agreed upon policy and procedures for running the practice. These agreements indicate who makes decisions about which issues and how these decision makers proceed while they are in process of deciding. Even very small firms or family partnerships need an explicit decision-making policy in writing. This is a precaution against misunderstandings. It also formalizes the importance of this vital practice function.

When a partnership runs smoothly, written guidelines seem unnecessary. It is during times of personal stress, overwork, financial crisis or major project development that a partnership needs the guidance which a written agreement provides. It also serves as a training document for new partners, associates, juniors and support staff because it presents a summary of 'how things are done' within the practice. The time, attention and care which partners bring to their decisions provide insight into their priorities and the firm's leadership style. Both autocratic or permissive leaders (see pages 61 and 62) are least likely to work with a written policy for decision making although their behaviour would result from very different attitudes.

A written policy implies a commitment to consistent decision making and to the relationships which form the partnership. It also protects individual partners from disenfranchisement or exclusion from decisions. This policy should form part of a longer *Partnership Agreement* which expresses the essential wishes of all of the partners. This is a statement of practice policy addressing all aspects of managing the firm. Decision making is one important area to be included in this document and there are nine others. The ten recommended areas are each described in the following paragraphs.

The ten issues highlighted here are likely to be included already in the firm's present Partnership Agreement. If they are not, then the partners can elect to discuss these points when their agreement is next revised. The points raised below are to stimulate debate among partners about their current thinking on these issues. This section is not intended as a substitute for legal advice. Appendix II provides reference information about governmental acts regulating partnership. Because a partnership is a business relationship recognized by law, specialist legal advice should be obtained when writing a Partnership Agreement.

Regular review of the Partnership Agreement is necessary, particularly when new partners join the firm. If this document becomes out of date, that is, its terms cease to reflect the current operation of the firm, then its validity can be questioned. This is particularly so when the document also lacks the signatures of partners who newly join the firm. Even if they sign a document stating that they will honour the terms of the Partnership Agreement, this is not necessarily binding if the agreement's terms have changed over the years. The partnership in this case becomes, by default, a *partnership at will*. This means that any partner can call for the dissolution of the partnership at any time and require an equal distribution of its assets.

The Partnership Agreement is so essential an issue that it needs to receive proper attention. The best time to review its contents is when there is harmony within the firm. During times of stress or strained relationships a clear agreement is needed, but these are also the times when it is virtually impossible to formulate it. By giving appropriate attention to their legal and fiscal relationship, partners establish a foundation for their professional work together. When trouble arises, they have a foundation upon which to make sound decisions and create resolution.

Ten essential topics

Shared workload and income

A definition should be provided for what constitutes income for the practice. This should include reference to partners' earned income from outside the firm and a policy covering a range of eventualities. Issues should include performance-related pay, non-professional work interests and professional work conducted outside the firm. New partners should have a clear understanding of their partners' expectations. Any inequity concerning workload should be addressed with a policy about earning parity. It is wise to include a clause stating that partners should give full-time attention to the practice, where this is the case, with outside pursuits that intrude into that time needing the consent of the partners.

Restrictive covenants

This refers to the protection of the firm's established custom, its 'brass plate' restrictions which limit an outgoing partner from setting up a rival practice within the local environs of the firm and from soliciting the firm's existing clients. Caution must be used here because any seeming valuation of 'goodwill' could cause tax problems. This area must be thoroughly discussed with a legal adviser.

Income disbursement

This section should provide guidelines for partners' drawings, incentives for training, promotion of the practice and new business acquisition, bonuses, equity reinvestment and profit sharing. In specific terms, the system of shares should be set out with a clear description of progression to parity among partners.

Leave arrangements

This should describe how many partners can take leave at one time, limits for time away and legitimate reasons for this leave, such as a holiday, illness, study, parental leave and partner-consented pursuit of outside interests.

Maternity leave and extended illness

Maternity leave should be on a par with leave granted for extended illness. Female partners can construe any seeming financial penalty for pregnancy as sex discrimination. The equitable nature of maternity leave arrangements should be made explicit, as well as any limits for coverage of extended illness.

Practice assets

This should list all capital assets, including equipment, facilities, premises, cash and investments. If the premises are owned by the firm, all partners should understand how their holdings have been computed. There should also be an agreement about valuation of all property. This gives outgoing and incoming partners clear information about what the transfer of their share in the practice actually means. As well, where a firm has a well-developed computer system and partners actively use and contribute to its database, the ownership of any data held by the practice needs to be clearly defined. Electronic memory makes it possible for an outgoing partner to carry away the equivalent of a lorryload of paper files in a small plastic case. Information is a practice asset and this needs to be made explicit.

Ending the partnership

The reasons for ending a partnership should be outlined. This includes voluntary and involuntary retirement, expulsion, the periods of notice and the procedure for transferring partnership share on leaving. For the UK the Partnership Act of 1890 (see Appendix II) states that a partner cannot be expelled from the partnership unless the partnership agreement addresses this issue. This clause in particular requires legal advice.

Conflict

If decision making breaks down despite clear policies and procedures, there should be a provision for mediation. This includes reference to a neutral party or organization as a source of arbitration. The issue of conflict resolution is easily discussed when there is peace within the practice. It is virtually impossible to create an arbitration policy once serious conflict develops.

Decision making

The kind and magnitude of decisions requiring the full approval of the partnership should be defined in terms of their potential impact on the practice: its reputation, future, finances and other essential issues. Also, the preferred methods for decision making should be described. Options include: formal or informal debate, open discussion and the optional use of a moderator. Another key area is explaining what constitutes a final decision. Options include: a defined quorum of majority versus minority or a requirement for consensus agreement.

It helps to include a provision for asking dissenting minorities if they are willing to go on record as a 'loyal minority'. This means they will act upon and support the majority's decision fully, but are recognized within the minutes as having disagreed. This is more than a face-saving exercise. Asking dissenting partners if they are *willing* to be a loyal minority invites them to be part of the decision, shows respect for their willingness to debate and avoids ignoring their position. All of this leads to greater unity of action.

If they are unwilling to be a loyal minority, then the debate is not concluded. Forcing a decision on partners who do not agree only causes their resistance to go underground. Their admission of such strong dissent is actually a gift to their partners who can then ask: What assurance do you need to at least say that you will be a loyal minority? The debate should continue until this assurance is defined and a loyal minority agreement is obtained.

Procedures

Procedures are those actions which implement policy. They ease the running of the firm because routine matters are automatically addressed by procedure. Too little procedure leads to chaos and overloaded decision-making sessions. Too much creates bureaucracy and a restricted ability to respond to unique or special situations.

Where there are clear agreements, policies and procedures, the practice avoids 'reinventing the wheel' whenever a decision must be made. There are firms which enter into debate about *regularly recurring* issues, as if each case were unique and required the full attention of the practice. When there is agreement, then policy statements readily follow because the thinking and feeling of the partners can be clearly represented.

TOOLS AND TECHNIQUES

Language bias

Skilful leaders are often sceptical and challenging when making decisions, but then confident and determined when executing them. Analysis of information requires questioning, exploration of doubts, insistence upon discussion and rigorous challenging of preconceived ideas. This approach provides an open-minded assessment of the issues. Even so, once the decision is made, the continued expression of doubt and scepticism undermines the potential success of the decision. Complete and positive commitment is the appropriate and responsible attitude to implementation of an agreed decision. At issue then is how to choose a specific option so that feelings of doubt have been addressed as fully as possible.

Max Bazerman, an American academic has researched the importance of words and phrases when presenting options for decision making. His work suggests that when a specific choice seems to promise a *definite outcome*, that is, there is no risk involved, people choose an option that is phrased in positive terms. Alternatively, when a choice seems to promise only a *probable outcome*, that is, there is a risk involved, they choose an option phrased in negative terms. This process is illustrated in the following example.

Example

A firm of solicitors is being sued by a client for purported conflict of interest. They anticipate that it will cost the firm as much as £50 000 if the suit is lost in court. They also know that the client will accept a £25 000 settlement. Having analysed their situation in terms of previous court decisions and met with their former client, they believe that they have two options:

1 settle out of court and definitely lose £25 000 in payment
2 go to court and face a 25 per cent probability of losing £50 000.

Alternatively, these options can be phrased in the following way:

A settle out of court and definitely save £25 000 in payment
B go to court and face a 75 per cent probability of saving £50 000.

Research findings suggest that partners are likely to choose option 2 over option 1 in the first set, and option A over option B in the second set. Interestingly, options 1 and A describe the same alternative, but are phrased differently, as do options B and 2. The difference is in linking negative language to risk-associated situations, and positive language to risk-free situations.

Partners who wish to limit this kind of bias should present decision-making options carefully. Options that offer a *definite outcome* should be presented so that *positive terms* are used, as in option A. Options that offer a *probable outcome* should be presented so that *negative terms* are used, as in option 2. In this way, bias about the options' phrasing is minimized so that the choices can be better evaluated *on their merit*.

To illustrate this, decisions can be presented so that greater care is taken when comparing options which promise a *definite* outcome against those which offer a *probable* one. In the court settlement example, options A and 2 could be compared so that issues of this kind of language bias are addressed:

A settle out of court and definitely save £25 000 in payment
2 go to court and face a 25 per cent probability of losing £50 000.

Because bias is a serious cause of concern for decision makers, wherever possible their effects should be kept to a minimum.

Decision-making methods

There are decision-making systems available which focus on rational as well as non-rational methods. Non-rational methods include intuition, divination and dice throwing, among others. There is also a highly distinguished and international group of theorists who proposes that all decision making is, in fact, 'irrational'. These include some advocates of chaos theory as well as those who recognize the extreme ambiguity which attends managerial decision making. The latter group refers to their approach as 'garbage pail thinking'.

Many leaders use a non-rational approach when they are pressed to make decisions about complex issues, rapidly with barely enough time to consider the basic facts. Although a fascinating topic, non-rational methods defy inclusion in a 'tools and techniques' section such as this. Instead, attention is given here to rational approaches. The majority of these suggest that rational decision making requires a progression through the following stages.

The Rational Decision Making Process

- define the problem
- list the requirements for a solution
- decide the relative importance of the requirements' criteria
- generate options, explore possibilities to meet the requirements
- evaluate choices against the criteria
- make a final decision.

This allows a logical progression from a general field of information to a precise and specific decision based on an analysis of that information. These steps are particularly valuable when making major decisions. Referring to the decision-making criteria which the partners outline in their Partnership Agreement, they should all participate fully in every stage of this process with a moderator to guide the process if necessary. Every major decision requires this degree of time and attention.

Expert systems

This refers to computerized decision making. When computer technology first became widely available, there were enthusiasts who promoted its use for management decision making, believing that this would allow development of a purely rational approach. Unfortunately, experimentation shows that a computer cannot be programmed (as yet) to make decisions that require a consideration of values or risk tolerance. Major decisions requiring this kind of consideration need human analysis.

Even so, if an expert system is available to the practice, it does help decision makers to study all options thoroughly from a purely rational point of view. The computer-chosen rational solution therefore indirectly highlights the partners' biases and value judgements which potentially cloud their selection process. Used as a means to discover hidden priorities and preferences, an expert system's chosen option can provide a benchmark for discussion of risk, values and emotional bias.

PROBLEM – ANALYSIS – DISCUSSION

Problem

A firm of construction engineers began 15 years ago with just four partners. Since that time, one partner retired, another left for a prestigious position within government, and seven additional partners joined the firm. The two remaining original partners shared 40 per cent of the firm's equity and the seven newer partners divided the remaining 60 per cent equally among themselves. One of the founders was the elected managing partner and at least half of his time was spent on the administration of the practice. The other founder-member suffered from serious ill health and struggled just to maintain contact with his diminishing list of clients.

From long habit the two original partners often met privately to discuss practice business. Based on their discussions, the managing partner would make decisions for the firm. Although the firms' Partnership Agreement required that all decisions be discussed 'fully and frankly' among all of the partners, many decisions were made without consulting even a partnership majority.

One highly contentious issue was partners' drawings which were determined by the managing partner. The Partnership Agreement set guidelines for this issue, but these addressed the needs of the four original partners and had not been followed for at least eight years. As well, none of the seven newer partners had been asked to sign this agreement and no revision to this document had ever been made.

Recently, three partners who had joined the firm as juniors shortly after it was founded, met to discuss their dissatisfaction. They felt increasing frustration because they generated most of the firm's income and yet received relatively little reward. One of the three said that she was so angry at times that she wanted to leave the firm. In response, another pointed out that they were a 'partnership at will' and that if she chose, she could dissolve the whole partnership just by saying that she wished to do so. He explained that by not revising their Partnership Agreement, nor signing it, this had happened to the firm by default. Half joking, he asked his colleagues if they were frustrated enough to dissolve the firm and watch all of its assets sold. This idea amused his two partners and the meeting ended with their deciding to make a greater effort to reorganize the practice along more equitable lines.

Unfortunately just a few days later, the seriously ill partner requested an emergency meeting where he announced that he was retiring. After thanking his partners for their support, he added that his son who had been an associate for the last three years would assume full partnership and receive his father's 20 per cent share of practice equity. The son was a full ten years younger than the most youthful of the current partners.

The stunned silence was broken by one of the partners suggesting that they should discuss the idea fully and then vote. When the managing partner impatiently insisted that the decision had been made, one of his colleagues quietly but firmly said, 'Let the record show that I now move to dissolve this partnership'.

Analysis

1 The following features were damaging to the firm. Please list them in order of significance from 1 to 7 (1 is the highest degree of damage and 7 the lowest).

- out-of-date Partnership Agreement   —
- lack of decision-making structure   —
- nepotism   —
- ignorance of partnership law   —
- an 'us' versus 'them' situation among partners   —
- policy of control by two over seven partners   —
- repressed resentment and feelings of inequity   —

2 What is the likely response of the two founding partners to the demand for the dissolution of the firm?

3 What, if anything, could be done to save this firm from dissolution?

Discussion

This firm is a partnership in name only. Its two founding members give little attention to those management issues described in Chapter 2 under the heading 'Long-term leadership' (see page 26). They abuse their positions of power and deny their partners an opportunity to contribute to the firm's decisions. While there is no malevolence in the founders' behaviour, they are certainly incompetent managers. They also seem to be entirely unaware of their potential vulnerability. Because the Partnership Agreement is out of date, their continued status, income and influence depend upon the goodwill and tolerance of their seven partners.

Particularly when very large sums of money are involved, this is unwise. Although each new partner signed a statement to abide by the firm's guidelines, this is not binding if, first, the Partnership Agreement guidelines are out of date, and, second, if the partners have not signed the Partnership Agreement. Given the founding partners' lack of awareness and management skills, it is unlikely that they will be able to recognize the significance of their colleagues' statement of dissolution. The discussion that follows is likely to be acrimonious with rigid positions being taken on both sides. Depending upon the personalities of the firm's partners, this could mean an end to their professional relationships.

The practice needs new leadership, a new agreement, a forum for discussion, and policies and procedures for making decisions. Without a willingness to create this, it is perhaps better for the firm as it currently exists to dissolve. It is an untenable situation to be legally bound by partnership and yet lack enfranchisement for its decisions.

SUMMARY

This chapter points out the similarities between giving professional advice and making business decisions. It also describes two approaches to organizational structure, hierarchy and the matrix models, with background information and applications for professional firms. A third organizational structure, network management, is recommended which combines features of the other two. A process approach to decision making is defined and the crucial importance of having clear policies and procedures is highlighted. Ten important points for inclusion in a Partnership Agreement are presented and partners are encouraged to review their agreement as changes within the practice occur. Language bias and decision-making methods are also presented.

6

Finance

WHO IS MINDING THE STORE?

Regular discussion of practice finance allows partners to contribute insight into the management of the firm's resources. Even so, many partners resist participating in this important business activity. Although they recognize that financial management is their responsibility, they often delegate important decisions to their financial advisers. This is a successful strategy if they also examine essential financial figures regularly and take appropriate action as required. However much they delegate, partners are still entirely responsible for minding their own store. This chapter highlights those management areas essential for making informed financial decisions.

Occasionally, finance partners and practice accountants forget that many of their technically expert professional partners have just basic financial management skills. Those with rudimentary financial expertise typically do not know what they do not know. Specialists who wish to encourage these colleagues to participate more in managing the business help by giving them simplified reports and eliminating financial jargon.

In well-managed firms, finance partners play an important leadership role. Often their task is to show strength of will when their partners refuse to recognize financial constraints or to cooperate with budget agreements. On these occasions, the finance partner provides the voice of common sense and presses the case for responsible management in such a way that rebellion becomes indefensible. This role is most challenging in firms where partners make legally binding agreements and financial commitments on behalf of the firm without first gaining their colleagues' informed consent. The finance partner's task is to remind autocratic or individualistic partners that they need to gain approval from *all* of the *practice owners* before committing any practice resources.

Even in a small firm, the role of the managing partner should be distinguished from that of the financial manager. This ensures two distinct points of view when making important financial decisions. If none of the partners have financial skills, then this expertise should be brought into the firm from outside. In small firms, this support can be part-time as long as the source of advice is consistent and addresses issues of budget, cash, capital, investment, costing and target setting in a thorough manner.

The successful practice responds to financial issues as they arise with skill and flexibility. This means that communication between those who offer information and those who receive it must be excellent. Gaps in partners' understanding of financial issues are best addressed before errors arise and well in advance of a crisis. On occasion, financial partners must take on the role of educators as well as guardians of practice resources. Because many adults dislike feeling as if they are being taught, this offers considerable challenge. The finance partner or practice manager who promotes a general understanding of finances with tact and diplomacy contributes a great deal to the firm's success. Once partners decide what kind of information they need in order to make informed financial decisions, then their adviser can generate this data for them in the form of regular reports. This leads to the development of financial reports which are both read and understood.

CASE STUDY: PRIDIE BREWSTER CHARTERED ACCOUNTANTS

The purpose of this case study is to highlight those areas of financial management which are essential for creating a successful practice. The partner featured here describes how financial controls actually serve the partners' human needs as well as their professional requirements.

'Financial management is a human issue as well as facts and figures', says Mei Sim Lai, partner at Pridie Brewster Chartered Accountants. 'Partners must decide what they are after. They should ask themselves: Do we wish to build a strong practice which gives us a good income and pays us out when we retire, or do we want to develop a firm which we can sell for a capital sum? This means that partners must look to the future to see where their firm is headed.

'Not enough firms have proper financial systems producing good financial information. Many partners do not understand the figures they are given and then do not question them. There is a gap in the education of professionals. Reading a set of accounts is not difficult, but many professional people switch off when they see figures. They have a mental block. Part of the problem can be that too many figures are presented *at them*. A better approach is to present in a clear and simple form the key control figures needed to run the business.'

She explains that the partners who manage the firm must determine what financial information they need and how often they need it so that they can make timely and well-informed decisions. 'Financial information is only of value if it prompts action. Many professionals are not fully aware of how the different parts of their business affairs fit together.'

Essential tasks for partners are the setting of financial targets for the practice and development of a budget. Mei Sim suggests, 'A firm should set a target for income to be produced during the year from existing clients and from new business. Because there are likely to be bad debts, this should also be taken into account when the target is set. At the same time, the partners should also set a target for how much productive (fee-earning) time they must achieve in order to meet the financial target. This is their level of productivity.' A low financial target means a low need for income production, just as a high target requires high productivity throughout the practice.

Partners need to know if practice income is meeting the targets and also whether individual practice members are performing well in terms of producing this income. These two essential pieces of information guide partners in taking action: to speed up billing, to go after bad debts, to revise budgets, to attract new business, to improve productivity, to change charge-out rates, among many other issues. The timely review of income and performance reveals potential difficulties so that these can be resolved before they become crises.

'The firm needs a system for looking at monthly accounts and seeing how materially different they are from budgeted figures', says Mei Sim. 'It would be the job of the managing partner to look at this in detail. Partners must agree to budget figures and there must be ownership. Each year they should tell the managing partner their requirements and then these figures should be organized so that they make sense. The budget as a whole should be approved by all the partners year by year and then reviewed every six months, or sooner if things go astray.' When partners do not either understand or agree to a budget, then this can lead to lack of cooperation, or, even, serious administrative error.

Mei Sim says, 'Control of income and expenses requires looking ahead. If there is a big tax bill coming up, then it is unwise to use available cash to make capital purchases. Partners should look at the way in which a big expense should be financed and avoid creating cash-flow problems. This is tied up with making full use of all available resources and getting maximum return on invested surplus cash. The partners must review whether they have sufficient capital to run the business. Without accurate figures, for example, partners can continue to have high drawings when the profits are not there. Then they get into trouble with the banks and their creditors.'

If partners discover that the firm's income is below their target, then they should either increase the amount of business the firm conducts or increase the fees charged for their services if there is reason to believe they are undercharging. Costs and overheads also need to be reviewed. She explains, 'There is a formula which many firms use. This is to charge 2.5 to 3 times what the professional costs the firm in terms of salary, pension, company car and so forth. Given an adequate level of business, this multiple provides for overhead and creation of profit. Professionals sell their time at a value. Therefore, for them, time really is money. They need a sophisticated time recording system in place.

'At Pridie Brewster, we have been computerized for a long time. Recently we switched to recording our time daily. This is a lot more accurate because we record everything in six-minute units, and our time sheets are authorized daily. It's also time-saving because each section's secretary posts the time to the ledgers. This system gives clients an accurate breakdown of information and also allows us to bill faster and get paid faster, too. Alternatively, there are firms which charge on a basis of their perceived value of the work. Some may look at the number of the letters sent or the complexity of the case and then bill based on this. They can find themselves in some difficulty if the client challenges the bill.'

There are many issues to consider when creating financial controls. For professionals, there is also an issue of balancing commercial concerns with professional ethics. Mei Sim describes this dilemma in the following way, 'There is a fine line between professionalism and commercialism. For example, if a client is in trouble, a commercial decision would mean not having anything further to do with them. As a professional, ethics leads you to help the client because you cannot abandon people when they need you most. A benefit from this is client loyalty, professional reputation and work satisfaction. At the same time, you also have got to remember that you are in business and cannot put the client first at your own expense. Balancing these issues provides the basis for sound commercial management. This allows better decisions to be made about giving high-quality service to clients.'

PARTNERS' INVESTMENT

In a recent newspaper interview, the founder of a leading American accounting firm said that he chose to enter his profession after the Second World War because he understood that he would only need to buy a pencil and paper to begin a successful practice. In principle, of course, this is true because all professional activities are essentially labour-intensive. Financial reward directly results from effort made, for the most part, with pencil and paper or their 'high tech' equivalent.

In practice though, professionals are first required to establish themselves within a business framework: as self-employed traders or as employees or partners in a professional firm. The first of these, self-employment, is frequently perceived to be an attractive business option and yet it requires considerable initial investment and a realistic assessment of risk. A professional should ask whether money invested in a start-up firm would bring a better financial return if invested elsewhere. Unfortunately, the wish for independence through self-employment often influences an ambitious professional's decision making. It is also very difficult for individuals to view their own skills as a potentially bad investment.

The second option, employment or partnership in a firm, is by far the more conventional career path with potential movement from junior to senior to salaried partner to equity partner. Even in early career days, the majority of professionals set an objective of achieving partnership. This goal is so attractive that the required sum for the eventual investment in equity seems more like a fee for the privilege of partnership. Needless to say, it is not. It is an investment like any other, and professionals should ask themselves: Is the management of this firm good enough to make a significant investment of my capital a worthwhile venture? Furthermore, will there be a return on this investment that is at least in line with alternative investment opportunities?

Because a capital sum should work for its owner, professionals who invest in the firm's equity, as well as commit their time and energy to the business, are entitled to an appropriate return. This benefit is available when the firm's profits, after taxation, allow a substantial contribution to:

- a fund of cash to be held in reserve for slow periods or emergency
- increased need for cash if the firm expands (this should cover gaps in income from unbilled work in progress and short-term debt from suppliers)
- reward of partners for their expertise and the personal investment they make to sustain their standing within their profession
- repaying partners for the risk they carry as investors in the business.

The remainder of this chapter proposes that firms be managed so that there is a return on investment which contributes substantially to these four areas.

GAPS AND BUDGETS

Chapter 4, Vision and planning, defines targets and forecasts (see page 80) and proposes that practice goals in five business areas should be developed so that they fill the gap between the firm's future vision and its current reality. This chapter also suggests that partners are best advised to agree, first, to a vision for the practice and then produce a mission statement. Based on this, they can then set a financial target for at least a five-year time span. This gives every partner a shared and *measurable* reference point so that they can watch their firm's growth year by year. They also plan how to achieve their target by sharing goals for client service, marketing, human development, facilities management as well as financial management.

If the firm's income falls below the agreed target, then this seriously affects the partners' ability to achieve all of their goals. Any shortages in earned income should be identified immediately so that practice expenses can be adjusted accordingly or other actions taken. Mei Sim Lai (see page 150) emphasizes the importance of partners' receiving timely and accurate financial information about their firm's income and expenses. Although the rationale for this is obvious to those with some financial expertise, some partners do benefit from an explanation.

Regular financial reports allow partners to look at their *actual income* and *actual expenses* and then compare these amounts to the targeted income. These figures highlight exactly what the firm can afford to spend and also what it needs to earn during the year. Ideally, partners are able to glance at a financial report and see immediately if their actual spending exceeds the target or their actual earning is below the target. This is their signal to take immediate action toward correcting this situation.

The information for a financial report is drawn from the firm's *budget.* This is a word and concept which can have an adverse effect on many professionals. Although an essential practice discipline, the budget carries an association of tiny numbers listed in columns which inevitably lead to restriction, self-denial and earnest common sense. 'Save during good years to pay for lean ones.' A budget is generally acknowledged to be a grim necessity rather than a salutary means for achieving life-long ambitions.

This is interesting because the word's original usage was domestic and entirely neutral. 'Budget' made its first appearance in fifteenth-century written English in reference to a 'bag, pouch or wallet usually of leather'. By the eighteenth century, it gained the additional meaning of 'speaking one's mind', that is, opening one's budget. During that period, the Chancellor of the Exchequer when presenting the annual report to Parliament was said 'to open his budget' or, in other words, to divulge all pertinent information.

Throughout these development years, 'budget' continued to refer to a bag or pouch, so that an individual's 'money budget' held the amount of cash that person had to spend. It should be noted that the concept of an overextended budget is an entirely modern one. Formerly, when the budget was empty, this meant that the money was gone.

The demands of current professional life require sophisticated financial systems, and budgets are now closely associated with financial complexity. In popular usage, the budget literally refers to columns of figures and implies sleep-inducing calculations. This development is unfortunate because a budget is and should be far more than figures. It is, after all, the summary of all of the decisions which partners make about spending money. An image of gold coins measured from a leather pouch: one for rents, one for salaries, one for rewards, offers a far more accurate meaning for the term than lists of numbers on a page.

For example, partners who are responsible for individual departments submit an estimate to their colleagues for the department's annual expenses and income. Although this task is routine, it is also a first and vital step to achieving the partners' vision for the future. In the midst of allocations for paper supplies, telephone calls and working lunches are the signs that colleagues are honouring the goals of the practice. How people spend money shows what they believe to be important. The budget is *the means* to signal a need for discussion of differing values and, therefore, it is an excellent source for creating greater unity among the partners.

Partners should examine the firm's budget closely when it is initially prepared for the following year. If, for example, training is emphasized during planning sessions, then the budget should indicate how colleagues intend following through on this goal. Studying the budget for discrepancies between intention and action, at times, can cast colleagues in a harsh light. On occasion, partners produce budgets out of habit or as a 'reheated' version of last year's figures. They need to be reminded that the firm's overall goals are reflected in the way they elect to spend practice money. Potentially, this leads to further discussion of goals and values, and partners either reinforce their planning commitments or alter their decisions about goals.

Budget reports are best studied at the end of each month. Every department, or each partner in small firms, presents a brief summary of their actual income and expenses. Next to these figures, the budgeted estimates are shown. Ideally, a single glance at this short report shows the firm's financial progress. Use of a computerized system makes this information readily and easily available.

This report can also include information about the amount of available cash as well as the firm's outstanding short- and long-term debt. It is valuable for partners to see the extent of uncollected fees for the firm as a whole as well as for each department. When this information is seen against the firm's own borrowings, partners have an added impetus to pursue the collection of unpaid bills, either personally or indirectly through staff. The awareness that the firm is overdue payment of £10 000 by a client, and *as a direct result*, partners pay overdraft interest on a short-term debt of at least that amount leads more readily to action than does a memo from the managing partner.

WHAT PROFESSIONALS COST THE FIRM

Each professional costs the firm money in terms of salary, partners' drawings, perquisites, tax contributions and a portion of the overhead costs for running the firm. The details of these costs provide partners with information for deciding which clients, projects and cases are most profitable and which level of professional should complete the work. Although this information is not necessarily the only guide for decision making, it is very important and contributes to overall financial success.

In larger firms, the finance partner or manager provides partners with a specific analysis of the cost of each professional. In small firms, partners can estimate this amount very easily themselves. First, they extract from the firm's total expenses any amounts apportioned to fee earners as salary, drawings, perquisites, tax and any other individual expenses, but excluding amounts paid as profits. In professional firms, the remaining expenses are typically its *operating costs* which include the salaries and costs of maintaining support staff.

The figure for the firm's *total operating costs* is then divided by the number of business days in the year to estimate the *daily cost of operating the firm*. This figure can be further divided by the number of fee-earning members so that a share of the firms' daily operating cost can be assigned to each professional. The total cost of each fee-earning member includes this share of the firm's operating expenses, plus individually allocated amounts for salary, perquisites, and so forth.

An argument could be made that support staff and managers should also be included in the calculation for a share of overhead. After all, everyone uses light, heat, paper, office facilities and equipment, and so everyone equally creates operating costs, including support staff. Although democratic, this approach defeats the usefulness of the calculation. Fee earners provide the firm with the income to pay the overhead; support staff do not. Therefore, the burden of carrying a share of overhead rests with those who are actually required and able to produce income which is then used to offset operating expenses. If administration managers or support staff are included in the calculation, this lowers the average share of overhead each fee earner is required to bring into the firm.

It could also be argued that partners create more overhead than juniors or that firm members often have different-sized offices and so use varying amounts of electricity and disposable goods. It is certainly possible to calculate to a fraction of a pfennig each fee earner's exact share of overhead, and firms which have sophisticated computer software systems can readily achieve this, but for those who lack this facility, a more general figure for share of overhead is adequate.

Having a figure for costs of each professional which includes a share of overhead allows partners to estimate very quickly the potential costs of a project. When negotiating fees, this is useful because it eases calculations and leads to a more informed discussion when clients ask for concessions or fee modification.

CHARGE-OUT RATES

Mei Sim Lai (see page 150) proposes that professional firms should set their charge-out rates by multiplying what each professional costs the firm by a factor of at least three. This allows creation of profit and also covers hidden costs. Firms with highly paid professional members in expensive offices obviously need to set higher charge-out rates than firms with lower costs. Otherwise, after expenses are paid, there is nothing left as profit for the partners. Even so, fees have an impact on clients, and firms with very high rates *potentially* lose business to competing firms.

Aubrey Wilson, in *Practice Development for Professional Firms,* suggests that fees are best set with an awareness of both potential competition as well as client demand. He proposes several methods for determining fees, including the following:

- **Contingency payment** These fees are contingent upon a specific service being completed or performed. Litigation lawyers in the US receive a percentage of the litigants' reward on successful completion of the suit. Researchers, mediators and estate agents also use this method.

- **Fixed rates** These fees are set by a government body, chartering agency or other controlling organization.

- **Contract** These fees are by arrangement with specific clients and are influenced by work volume, long-term commitment or status of the work.

- **Value based** These fees reflect the value which clients place on a service or 'what the market will bear'.

There are other influences which should also be considered when making decisions about fees. These include:

- the 'normal' range of fees for the firm's location and specialisms
- the quality of service and professional expertise which the firm offers
- the degree of client affluence or their willingness to pay for the firm's service
- the firm's expenses and targets for performance, income and profit.

Whatever the specific fees, the collected income should meet operating costs (salaries, rents and other overhead expenses) as well as produce enough profit after tax to give partners a healthy return on their investment. Accurate and up-to-date figures for past income production and expenses allow a realistic analysis of the firm's ideal fees. If partners discover that their need for income requires them to set unrealistic fees, then they benefit from reconsidering both expenses and fees.

If they decide to lower their fees, they have two obvious options: either they cut their expenses so that they lower their need for income or they work additional hours so that they achieve the necessary income at the lower fees. Alternatively, partners could decide to go ahead with the higher fees. If so, they should also enhance their present services or add new areas of expertise so that clients willingly pay above-standard fees.

TIME RECORDING AND BILLING

A well-organized system for recording time is another essential for any practice, and leads to accurate invoices being sent out in a timely manner. Clients in general are more accepting of bills which present the details of service clearly and which arrive while the memory of these services is still fresh. Although the specific details of time recording systems differ from firm to firm, the principle is the same for all. Each professional makes a note of the actual time spent on client work. Generally, this is formalized by the use of preprinted sheets so that professionals enter the date, the task, the client and the time.

Typically, professionals make notes to summarize their activities at intervals of 30 minutes.

Information from these time sheets is then posted to clients' accounts as early as the next day or on a weekly or monthly basis. In small firms, support staff post these amounts while in larger ones, the accounting department does it. Because the posted amounts are the basis for client billing, this information is required before invoices are sent. If time sheets are late, then bills are late and so are payments from clients. This is an unhealthy situation in terms of the firm receiving the cash it needs to stay in business.

Each firm should decide the length of their billing cycle, whether monthly or quarterly and then keep to this. It is much more efficient to have a regular date for producing all of the firm's invoices at the same time. For example, a firm which chooses to bill on the 15th of each month makes sure that all time sheet information is posted to the clients' accounts in time for billing on the 15th. When members of a firm all work toward the same billing deadline, this creates consistent and reliable procedures. A single comprehensive effort is made to summarize the billed-time, and then complete and mail invoices so that all payments fall due monthly from the same date. This also makes collection follow-up more efficient.

A time recording system serves other management needs as well. Included among these benefits are:

- the identification of actual time for work completion
- the provision of data for job tender estimates
- the indications of training needs when task completion seems slow
- the analysis of non-productive time as an aid to improving decisions about delegation and administration.

Electronic systems

Use of the computer for billing and record-keeping is increasingly common in professional firms (see page 239). Computer use offers important benefits for billing. First, professionals can easily watch the time they put into a project. This only requires pressing a key to call a file on to the computer screen. Second, they can monitor their achievement of performance targets. The total amount of each professional's billed time for a given period can be presented on screen so that members of a firm see immediately if they are producing the income the firm needs. Use of a computer makes time recording that much more valuable because this information can be presented rapidly and immediately on request.

Professionals who are highly resistant to use of the computer screen themselves can be given printed copies of this information on request by their support staff. The benefits of using a computer depend primarily upon two factors:

- do professionals actually fill in the required time sheets and
- is the data from these sheets regularly entered into the computer system.

If either of these tasks is given only half-hearted attention, then the information on file is both inaccurate and of minimal value when checking targets or producing invoices.

PROJECT COSTS

When tendering for large-scale projects, a careful analysis should be made of the time which was recorded for similar projects in the past. This study can reveal how much work of what kind was completed by which level of staff. For example, a summary of hours from a survey project at XYZ and Partners produces these figures:

- partners = 100 hours expended
- seniors = 400 hours expended
- juniors = 400 hours expended

This breakdown provides a basis for analysing the way in which time was apportioned so that more accurate forecasts can be made for future project requirements. It also shows what the project costs the firm in terms of the hourly costs of each professional. As described before, this cost includes a share for overhead expense, salary or drawings, perquisites, tax payments and any other costs. If Mei Sim Lai (see page 150) and other accountants' advice is followed, these cost figures are multiplied by a factor of at least three. Based on this, fees for each professional level at XYZ would be:

- partners = £40 × 3 = £120 per hour
- seniors = £25 × 3 = £75 per hour
- juniors = £10 × 3 = £30 per hour

If the firm wishes to make their future bids more competitive, partners at XYZ can first analyse the project's work needs to determine which level of staff is actually required to provide the client with quality service. They may decide that improved delegation and better efficiency would allow them to assign lower costing professionals to complete a greater part of the project than on the previous occasion. The proposed breakdown for a future bid could be:

- partners = 70 hours
- seniors = 410 hours
- juniors = 420 hours

By substituting more junior professionals in a controlled manner, they lower the cost *to the firm* for completing the project without undermining quality. They also lower the cost *to the client*.

As well, use of the firm's hourly fee rates for project bid tendering can create unrealistic or uncompetitive figures for billing clients for professional time. Depending upon the desirability of the project under tender, planners could also vary their use of a factor of three because the lower cost of professional time would substantially modify the bid. If they do this, they should first ask themselves what intangible benefits does the project offer which offset their lower profit margin. Obviously, winning a bid for a project which ends up costing the firm money is a mistake. This is where hard data from time recording is a valuable resource for decision makers.

CASH FLOW

When the system for billing runs smoothly, then the firm's earned income flows in smoothly. When it is blocked, inefficient or haphazard this inhibits the inflow of cash and eventually undermines the firm's viability. Ideally, there is a cycle for the flow of cash.

Client requests service	→	fees are earned	→	fees are billed	→	fees are received	→	firm pays own bills

If this cycle breaks down at any point, then the firm lacks the cash to pay its own bills. Some firms resort to taking short-term loans as a means to bridge this kind of financial difficulty. Others use an overdraft facility in order to maintain their ongoing expenses.

The former solution is often a planned decision. It typically occurs when partners recognize that they are about to face a large expense, such as a tax payment or a major purchase, and they lack the cash to pay for it. Then they either approach the bank for a loan or decide to borrow the money from members of the firm itself. In either case, they are in a position to look for a lower rate of interest.

Alternatively, the latter overdraft solution is often unplanned. It results from problems with fee collection, extensive amounts of unbilled work in progress, practice over-spending or professionals under-earning. When a firm depends upon an overdraft to pay its bills, then partners need to review their financial management. If they use an overdraft facility and yet have large fees uncollected or waiting to be billed, they are cheating themselves of the overdraft interest they are required to pay until these fees are collected.

Before commercial loans are assumed, partners should consider alternatives which provide lower interest rates. They can create their own internal 'bank', made up of contributions from the partners. The cash reserve which they create can be drawn upon whenever the firm falls short of cash. Contributions to this cash fund function as deposits to a savings account with an agreed rate of interest in line with current banking rates. The firm should also consider adding a premium to this interest. Those who support the idea enhance the firm's stability and, therefore, should be rewarded accordingly.

Alternatively, if a cash emergency arises, partners can voluntarily lower their drawings in order to cover unplanned expense. This solution best applies to cash crisis situations. In general, partners should receive a healthy return on their capital investment. If the firm is consistently in debt, this is negative capital, and partners should examine the effectiveness of their firm's management.

PERFORMANCE TARGETS

Although partners ultimately are the beneficiaries of performance targets, they are usually the most resistant to assuming these goals for themselves. Performance targets offer a guide that helps professionals focus on the amount of income they need to produce. Every partner should have targets for both *income production* as well as for *profit creation*. Although the two figures are linked, it is useful to distinguish *profit* from *earned income* so that partners recognize the need to watch expenses carefully. Even if earnings are high, there is no profit if expenses eat up everything that is earned.

It is tempting to rationalize liberal spending habits when earnings are up and business is good, but this attitude leads to minimum profits. To return to the image of the leather 'budget'. If as many gold coins are spent as are earned, then there are no coins remaining. Profits can be shared only when there is something left over in the money bag after all the expenses have been paid.

Another useful target is the generation of 'new' business. Some partners benefit from distinguishing between the income derived from existing clients and that from newly made contacts. Although both types of business are equally valuable, new clients mean that the practice is growing. This, in turn, leads potentially to new referrals and also replacements for those clients lost through natural attrition. Occasionally, an existing client requests new levels of service or additional specialist advice. It is difficult to determine when 'additional' means 'new'. Each firm should decide this individually when measuring their partners' achievement of set targets.

DRAWINGS AND REWARDS

Decisions about drawings and the timing of profit distribution are necessarily based upon the best available financial advice. It is obvious that partners deserve compensation for their professional effort as well as a healthy return on their capital investment through receipt of a share of the profit. The form taken for partners' drawings and rewards is then based upon the individual firm's overall capital needs, the division of equity, the degree of belief in performance-related pay and the value placed upon promoting the firm, training junior staff, administration and other non-fee-earning efforts. All of these are issues which should be discussed among the partners.

Salary criteria

Having said this, there are several points which can be applied to professional firms in general. For example, many firms are set up so that partners receive a regular salary, payable before the distribution of profits. Above their salary, they receive a share of the profit on a monthly, quarterly or annual basis. There is an advantage to considering salary as compensation for actual completed work because those who wish to assume an ambitious schedule in excess of the norms for the practice can be rewarded for this without necessarily causing resentment. The calculation of salary as a separate issue from distribution of profits, for some firms, offers a satisfactory solution for dealing with partners' individual work patterns. The following are a few possible criteria for deciding partners' salary:

General issues:

- how long in the firm
- how long a partner
- how many years active in the profession
- areas and extent of expertise
- amount of time given to essential practice administration
- degree of responsibility taken and number of people supervised.

Client activity:

- how many billable hours
- how many new clients or projects developed
- the size of client list
- total fee generation from direct work and supervision of others.

All of these features contribute to decisions about individual salaries. In contrast, profit would be based upon the equity held by each partner. If information about profit is available on a monthly basis, then a share can accompany payment of salary. This requires careful planning so that provision is also made for payment of unexpected expenses. A firm needs to maintain enough capital to cover operating costs as well as invest in its growth. Profit quickly becomes loss if partners receive large drawings and then need to borrow heavily to pay their expenses.

Perquisites

Perquisites is a challenging issue for many firms. A case can be made for providing partners with minimum perquisites in the form of expensive cars, modes of travel and offices. Because these expenses cut into the firm's profits, some partners want to keep such costs low and then make individual decisions about use of their subsequently higher profit-share. When partners have varying attitudes about expenses, this can lead to competition over who spends the most. For example, a partner who does not either want or need an expensive car may choose to have one if all of the other partners have them.

Because the cars are paid for or leased at the firm's expense, it is a tangible reward which would otherwise be profit. Any partner who goes without and yet receives no equivalent reward actually loses a share of practice profits. No one likes this and so expenses escalate as each partner insists on receiving what everyone else gets.

Alternatively, partners can receive a menu of 'priced' perquisites from which they select the rewards they most desire. This menu would be produced with awareness of the effect of tax liability on the value of one selection over another. This approach is called 'cafeteria-style' or 'menu' benefits in the US and Canada, and individuals are allocated an 'allowance' to spend on their menu selections. If practice leaders wish to cut partners' expenses to increase profits, then this approach to perquisites is one alternative for improving the firm's reward system. It certainly helps limit competitive spending and unnecessary resentment resulting for inequity.

PROBLEM – ANALYSIS – DISCUSSION

Problem

Seven years ago, four interior designers formed a partnership so that they would have greater credibility when tendering for corporate bids. In practice, the firm was loosely organized so that each partner ran a separate business unit but also operated under the partnership's name. The firm gradually grew to include 15 partners who shared the cost of leasing prestigious office space in proportion to their individual use. They also shared salary payments for clerical and other jointly hired support staff. At the same time, each partner was entirely responsible for the running of their own business unit with eight of these units employing associates on salary.

This arrangement worked well because the partners all brought a high level of goodwill to their business relationships. They often worked out financial and logistical matters over the phone or, if absolutely necessary, through an informal meeting of the whole partnership. One of the original partners was responsible for collecting and managing the 15 partners' contributions to the firm's upkeep, as well as coordinating their decision-making requirements. She billed the other partners for this administration time at her professional rates. When the firm began, her partners protested about this because her professional rates were very high for administration work. When she suggested that one of them take on the work instead, the subject was never raised again.

The first episode of real difficulty arose over a misunderstanding about associates' salary payments. One of the partners was generally recognized to be a thoroughly incompetent financial manager. Although his practice generated a very large income, he was always short of cash, and his business unit was in a state of perpetual chaos. Although this partner employed two highly skilled associates, he had no system for time recording. Quarterly billing always presented a crisis to his unit. Even so, these associates liked and respected their boss and were very loyal to him.

Six months before, a large lease payment fell due, and this partner was unable to pay his share. The practice manager stepped in and proposed that each of the partners contribute a portion of his unpaid share. In return, she suggested that his associates work for each of the partners in lieu of this payment. The cash-poor partner happily agreed to this.

Unfortunately, he did not grasp that this arrangement required him to continue paying the associates' salaries himself. He was shocked when he learned this and believed himself to have been tricked by the managing partner. As well, the 'loss' of his associates' time caused him to fall seriously behind on an important project. For the first time, bad feeling developed among the partners.

Although the two associates fully understood the financial terms of the arrangement, *they felt* very resentful about it. They disliked being used as currency in a barter exchange. Even so, they did not really know who to blame because everyone seemed to them to have acted in good faith. Because their unit lacked a system for time recording and even the will to set one up, the associates had no means of showing how many hours they worked for the other partners. In fact, one associate had repaid one partner at least double the value of the loan, 11 had been almost repaid and two partners had received no time contribution at all.

Analysis

1   What is the root cause of this present financial misunderstanding?

2   What does this practice need most in terms of financial management?

3   What is the likely result of this communication breakdown?

4   Who is responsible for this situation and what should the partners
     do to resolve it?

Discussion

This problem exaggerates the situation of partners who view
themselves and their clients' business as being independent of the rest
of the firm. They want the benefits of partnership but not the
responsibilities. The root cause of this situation is the partners' belief
that they can jointly accept financial liability without setting standards
for financial management. The firm lacks financial performance
criteria for its separate business units as well as a unified system for
managing jointly owned resources.

All of the partners know that at least one of their number has a weak
grasp of finance. They would have benefited this partner by insisting
that he hire a business manager to supervise his affairs. Because the
partners resist this kind of 'interference', they create an impossible
situation, that is, they have joint responsibility and yet no requirements
for accountability.

Given the volume of their work and the inevitable rise in the cost of
running the firm, the practice needs to monitor its operational
expenses. The partners should jointly decide a budget that meets these
needs and then hire a finance manager to supervise it. This manager
could also provide each business unit with regular reports about their
operational costs. Financial management standards could be established for all of the units and the manager could assist in organizing
those units which needed additional management service at the unit's
expense.

The present situation could certainly be resolved given the history of
goodwill which characterizes this firm. The partners need to meet
formally and discuss their difficulty. The firm is now too large and
central costs too high to continue without some form of financial
control and more formal management decision making. All of the
partners are jointly responsible for this situation, and its resolution
depends upon their finding a new balance between autonomy and
partnership.

SUMMARY

This chapter emphasizes the importance of every partner's participation in financial management. It suggests that the firm's financial plan be based on the partners' goals for the future. Reference is made to Chapter 4, Vision and planning, which discusses this issue. The chapter also addresses the need for regular financial reports. These should be short and yet give information which leads to immediate response and action where necessary. A method for calculating what the members of a practice cost the firm is proposed and it is suggested that this information be used to determine charge-out rates for professional services. The need for accurate time recording is discussed and issues of performance targets and financial rewards are also explored.

7

Practice development

PROMOTING NEW BUSINESS: A SCENARIO

During their monthly meeting, the managing partner of a firm of solicitors presents quarterly financial results to his ten partners. He highlights four points.

- income is 25 per cent lower than expected
- expenses are 15 per cent higher
- fee earning activity throughout the firm is 20 per cent lower
- income receipts are collected at an average of 60 days.

The partners realize that they must take immediate action because this situation, if ignored, could lead to serious financial problems. They decide that the heads of departments should:

- set in motion a fee collection drive in their departments
- make immediate cuts in the next quarter's expenses to remedy their present excess expenses
- emphasize to all professionals the importance of time recording and billing.

The determination and enthusiasm of the partners for this plan creates a positive and reassuring atmosphere. Only one partner, at the end of the meeting, points out that the budget problem in her department results from their having fewer requests for their services. This comment unsettles her colleagues. Silence falls, until the managing partner responds that her department simply will have to improve on that during next quarter. 'Get those billings up,' he says.

This scenario highlights the blind spot many professionals have about their individual responsibility for marketing their firm. Requests for service do not just happen. They result from clients making a choice to contact the firm. Even well-managed firms whose partners readily pull together toward a common goal can underperform because they do not recognize the need to develop their firms. This means encouraging current clients to stay with them, even as they generate additional business from new clients.

CASE STUDY: KENNETH LEVENTHAL & COMPANY

The purpose of this case study is to present an example of a firm with a highly successful development strategy. Those features which contribute directly to this success are highlighted so that application can be made to professional firms in general.

Kenneth Leventhal & Company specializes in providing accounting and consulting services to the property industry in the US. In 1989–90, each Leventhal partner generated average fees of $1.93 million which far exceeded the per partner totals of the world's six major names in accounting. It is the eleventh largest accounting firm in the world in terms of turnover. With only 74 partners, this is a significant achievement particularly because the firm only began in 1949 having been founded in a two-room Los Angeles flat.

It is also a founding member of Clark Kenneth Leventhal, an international association of independent firms with members from 45 countries providing a network for the firms' mutual support and benefit. Although the Leventhal process of growth and development is relevant to firms of any size, its approach offers special insight to small practices which seek a strategy for success.

Leventhal's strength is its reputation. Partners are highly committed and extremely hardworking. Their expertise and involvement in the property industry has led to their involvement in the creation, development and interpretation of virtually all specialized property audit and accounting rules that currently exist in the US. Because the firm's reputation emphasizes specialist property service, this leads banks, institutional investors and even the US Government to turn readily to Leventhal's when an independent enquiry is necessary.

One assignment in the late 1980s led to the preparation of a government report concerning the Lincoln Savings and Loan debacle and followed the firm's investigation into the widespread failure of the US savings and loan [building society] industry. The Leventhal report challenged several accounting transactions that Lincoln's auditors had formerly approved. Kenneth Leventhal, the firm's founder now in his seventies, acknowledges that, 'The people who ran the savings and loans weren't all crooks. Most of them were pillars of the community who followed the three-six-three rule: borrow at three, lend at six and at the golf course by three. Of course business isn't as simple as that, and that's why they went wrong. Personally, I blame the Government for allowing so many people to start small thrifts [savings societies] and insuring them.'

There are those who ascribe Leventhal's present growth to this banking crisis and the extensive work which the firm took on as a result. This ignores the difficulties which other accounting firms currently suffer even as Leventhal's continues to succeed. Kenneth Leventhal believes this success is based upon single-mindedness and conservatism. During the late 1980s when other firms chose to grow through merger, Leventhal's ran an advertisement saying, 'Merger? Not for us.' This made public their ongoing commitment to the firm's tradition of client service, guiding principles and integrity. It is also indicative of the firm's ability to remain focused on a niche market and resist expanding out of its specialist area.

The partners excel in what the firm calls 'work-outs'. This term refers to a process whereby borrowers who are experiencing financial difficulties get together with their lenders in order to reach an understanding, out of court, about the fair and equitable resolution of their loans. Kenneth Leventhal explains, 'Basically, these companies have a pile of assets and it's a matter of rolling around in the dirt to decide who gets more. We offer a non-judicial, consensual plan where we weigh the relative positions of debtors and creditors and prepare a plan to take into account their conflicts of interest.' Leventhal's works with those involved *to avoid* bankruptcy and enforced liquidation.

Instead, they develop a plan which recognizes asset value and repays debt.

Kenneth Leventhal believes that restructured debt in general offers a more beneficial approach for all concerned because judicial intervention is so complex and expensive. He says, 'From that basic premise stems our entire endeavour, but you have to know all the rules. That's the bar of soap that we sell.' It is perhaps this blending of skill and experience with a desire for a fair outcome which creates a demand for the firm's services. Stan Ross, the firm's managing partner says, 'When my client complains about how tough the banks were and the banks complain about what they left on the table [their concessions], I know the negotiation was successful.'

The firm's reputation is such that its partners have credibility as independent third parties, assessing all of the facts, including legal, tax and financial matters. Although they are known for their client-first approach and personal service, the firm's philosophy demands full disclosure of all assets from a client before taking on a work-out assignment. The partners are seen to consider all special interests with objectivity while also protecting their client's interests in the negotiation.

In fact, creditors themselves are known to recommend that their troubled debtors contact Leventhal's. Donald Trump, the American property developer and financier hired the firm at the strong recommendation of his banker. Stan Ross and his team are widely acknowledged for saving Trump from default on more than $300 million in bonds. The firm's credibility invites clients from virtually every interest group associated with property negotiation: developers, borrowers, investors, industrial owners as well as representatives of creditors' associations when a property deal runs into trouble. By providing objective advice, the partners help clients resolve financial difficulties and also build good relationships with those in potentially adversarial roles.

This firm illustrates that single-minded management, adherence to values and guiding principles, and commitment to client service leads to substantial growth in just one generation. Richard Klein, the firm's national partner for development and marketing says, 'A large firm can push in many directions all at once because it has the resources to do this. We have developed a niche market which allows us to focus our resources in one direction. This concept works well for us, but the truth is that there is no substitute for being technically smart and working hard.'

THE ECOLOGY OF COOPERATION

James Moore, a Massachusetts-based consultant proposes that technological advances have contributed to a radical change in the very nature of competition. He highlights the importance of market development through *networks*. These are clusters of individual businesses which cooperate to provide mutual support in a systematic way. This approach challenges the idea that marketing means a head to head contest with the opposition to win a client's business or acquire a project contract. Networking is a more subtle form of promotion so that new business results from shared interests and direct contact with a wide variety of industries and complementary professional services. These contacts are nourished through the regular exchange of ideas, knowledge and the pursuit of innovative ways to serve clients. Firms committed to networking are always willing to give leads and information to their contacts.

An example of this is the accountant who provides audit services to a research laboratory. On their request, this professional is able to recommend a trusted patent attorney. This becomes a network of three different disciplines cooperating in practice promotion. Over time as introductions continue, the network grows ever larger.

This approach to business development is certainly not new. It has been in existence since human beings began the barter of goods and services. It is of particular value in today's market-place because advances in computer technology have increased even a small firm's ability to link up with other professionals. As well, an active use of networks enhances the firm's ability to meet clients' specialized requirements. The firm that is known for expert service and also for its contacts within a range of disciplines and industries is very attractive to knowledgeable clients who value informal information sources. Today, access to a variety of sophisticated networks is an intangible but very important practice resource.

In contrast, the traditional professional firm works in relative isolation lacking the advantage of direct, if informal, contact with complimentary professional services. These firms gain new business primarily through referrals or chance meetings over a game of golf, squash or tennis. This approach to business development cannot really compete with a firm which actively contributes to business and professional networks. The latter has both the skill and contacts to gain personal introductions and direct referrals to decision makers. This kind of practice promotion is far from random and depends only partly upon luck.

Analysis 7

These questions should be completed by individual partners who can then discuss their answers together later.

1 Make a list of the firms with which your firm has a long-standing relationship. This can include clients, competitors, suppliers and others.

2 Ask each partner to list the number of business referrals they *gave* each of these firms during the last year.

3 List the number of referrals each partner gained from each of these firms during the last year.

4 Consider any other sources of new clients gained during the last year. List these.

5 Do any partners have a source of new client work in common? If so, how do they coordinate their contacts with each client?

6 Do any patterns emerge concerning sources of clients from certain industries or certain business activities?

7 Ask partners to discover patterns of client acquisition during the last year.

8 How can further contacts be made within these industries or through these activities by way of present contacts?

9 Consider what kinds of new business your firm can help these contacts obtain?

10 Set goals and objectives to achieve performance targets for new business (see page 92).

UNIQUE SELLING PROPOSITION

To gain the maximum benefit from participating in a network, a firm needs a strong identity so that it avoids merging into a multi-discipline soup. Giving and receiving support through links with other firms requires each business in the network to be individually robust. The section in Chapter 4 on vision (see page 82) suggests that partners ask themselves what they want the future to hold for the firm. It is proposed that they consider the *qualities* they believe are most important and relevant to their work. This process of examining the practice gives direction to the firm and common goals to the partners. It also contributes to the definition of the firm's unique selling proposition (USP).

USP is also referred to as 'distinctive competence',' market edge' or 'market advantage'. Essentially, it is a statement that identifies an important practice strength which *satisfies a demand* for service and which also *provides an advantage over the competition*. Although every practice has many strengths, the USP is a strength that emphasizes the firm's ability to meet a client demand in such a way that it gains the business and excludes the competition.

The discovery of the USP of a particular practice begins with the partners making an inventory of their firm's strengths. This list of strengths is then assessed in terms of how their clients actually respond to each of these. This evaluation frequently reveals that some of the features believed by the partners to be sources of major strength, in fact, are not relevant to client demand or do not distinguish the firm from its competition.

For example, a firm which prides itself on the educational background of its partners needs to determine if their pool of clients *values this* before it is selected as a USP. As well, if the competition has an identical strength, then this also disqualifies it as a specific advantage and, therefore, does not help to define the firm's USP. Essentially, the USP defines what makes the firm unique, special and different in terms of servicing the client.

Once the partners determine their USP, they have a powerful selling tool. It serves them when they speak to potential clients about the benefits of consulting their practice and also assists decision making throughout the firm. For example, when staff *know* that quality is a feature of the firm's USP, then they feel empowered to make choices which reinforce this in their work without having to check with higher authority. A clear statement of USP is another way to communicate to those inside and outside the firm the nature of practice priorities.

Unique, special and different

The following analysis activity leads to the development of a practice profile, and highlights those strengths which particularly meet client demands. This is a first step toward identifying the firm's USP.

Analysis 8

These questions should be completed by individual partners who then discuss their answers together.

1 What geographical area does the firm serve?

2 Who are its clients:

- which industries
- other professions
- government groups
- individuals (in terms of age, gender, background, career)?

3 Do clients request the firm's service:

- for routine work
- for specialist assignments

- for single projects
- for ongoing projects?

4 What are the firm's specialist areas?

5 Which clients do partners like to serve most?

6 What makes these clients attractive (identify actual causes: if the immediate answer is prompt payment, consider what enables the client to do this, for example is it well managed, in a cash-rich industry or is there another cause)?

7 What is it about the firm specifically which attracts or keeps these preferred clients?

8 What are the firm's qualities (see chapter 4, Vision and planning, page 84)?

9 How do these qualities particularly enhance client service?

10 How can these qualities create interest in the firm toward drawing new clients?

11 Summarize the features which most characterize the firm.

12 What are specific strengths that meet the clients' service demands?

The competition

Defining a firm's USP requires extensive knowledge and understanding of the competition. This information eases the process of distinguishing what makes a particular firm *different* and how it has an *advantage* as a result. At first, differences between competing firms can seem negligible to the partners. Those who are actively involved in managing the practice are often too close to allow development of objectivity or the necessary perspective. They need to take a 'mental step' back and examine their firm as if it were owned and operated by strangers. This is never an easy task, *at first*, and yet it is essential when determining what makes the firm unique, special and different.

Analysis 9 which follows leads to an assessment of the competition and, therefore, discovery of the firm's advantages. This is a second step toward identifying the firm's USP.

Analysis 9

These questions should be completed by individual partners who then discuss their answers together.

1 How many competing firms are there in the firm's own geographical area?

2 Of these, how many are:

- larger
- the same size
- smaller?

3 In general, what are the characteristics of:

- the large firms
- the same size firms
- the smaller firms?

4 Which specific firms constitute major competition?

5 Are there any competitors which offer a similar service to that of your firm or else serve very much the same specialist areas?

6 What kind of clients are drawn to these competing firms?

7 What, if anything, distinguishes these clients from the firm's own clients, in terms of their service requirements and other traits?

8 Summarize common characteristics of the competition. Include even those points that match the firm's own traits.

9 Examine this list closely to discover any points which are very different from the firm's, either in a positive or a negative way.

10 Look at the answers to item 12 in Analysis 8 (see page 180). Does the firm satisfy a client demand in any way that is different from the competition?

USP summary and assessment

Through discussion, partners gradually discover which markets they want and which they best serve. This allows them to clarify the kind of business the firm should seek: whether through its current network links or through new contacts which are yet to be made. The information summarized in Analyses 8 and 9 provides the basis for developing a practice USP. This statement then reinforces the firm's choice of markets.

In Chapter 4, there is an example of a firm of architects which develops a mission statement (see page 86). One result of this process is their choice of giving up time-consuming residential design work and seeking highly satisfying, and lucrative, industrial projects. Later, if these partners also choose to discuss USP, they would necessarily be influenced by this marketing decision. Just as their mission statement establishes the firm's general direction, their USP builds upon this. Its purpose is to present a short and sharp case to the client which promotes the firm and excludes the competition. For example, having studied their competitors and thoroughly examined their clients' needs in general, the architects could produce this USP:

> Our international award-winning designs create beautiful, practical and wholesome work environments.

This is the sequence to follow when developing a firm's USP:

1   list practice strengths
2   decide which of these directly meets a service demand
3   and also provides an advantage over the competition.

No matter how accurate and useful the firm's USP may be, it does need to be assessed regularly. Because actions from external forces, such as government, social values, competition, technology and client demands create conditions of almost constant change, firms must be prepared to adapt to this. Strengths in one situation can become liabilities in another. Obvious examples occur when changes in government policy lead to alterations of bidding requirements, or when a new competitor draws an important client away from the firm.

These situations are causes for partners to reconsider their firm in terms of these events. If they develop a new marketing strategy as a result, then this can mean revision of the firm's USP. Partners invest in success when they bring a flexible approach to evaluating their *current* strengths and regularly assess what makes their firm unique, special and different.

IMAGE

Having identified the USP, the partners' next task is to promote this as a feature of the firm's image. Before any decisions are made about practice promotion, it is best to gather information about the way in which the firm is currently perceived: by the public, by interest groups, by clients and by members of the firm itself. If there is a gap between the image which the firm wishes to project and the one which is currently held, particularly by clients, then action must be taken to close that gap.

Aubrey Wilson is an international authority on marketing for professional firms and is author of the first ever available book published on this topic. In a subsequent work, *Practice Development for Professional Firms*, he addresses the crucial issue of image.

> *The components which individually and collectively create the image of any professional activity, product or even ideology are very numerous when related to the professions. The client rarely makes a conscious separation of these components. What the client receives is an overall impression of the practice and its personnel which is the 'image profile'. No individual, no service and no product can avoid creating images and being assessed and evaluated on them. . . . images will develop irrespective of anything the individual or firm may do or not do. What is important is that firms should consciously seek to shape the image in a way which will help them achieve the practice development objectives. Images are not an aspect of practice development from which a firm can contract out. Their existence is as pervasive and as real as any tangible possession of the practice.*

(pp. 139–40)

He also remarks that the professions as a whole are currently seen in a relatively negative light by the general public, which perceives them to be arrogant, self-protective and very expensive. Although this general state of opprobrium is unfair and often unjustified, professionals who wish to promote a positive image of their firms need to be aware that they also face a public bias against professions generally as well as against their own profession specifically.

The image which the firm projects is received by a wide variety of audiences simultaneously, including its present clients, other firms within its profession, members of other professions, government agencies, banks, the firm's support staff, local businesses, neighbours in their office building and a myriad of others. Therefore, this general audience with all of these interest groups is a potential source of the firm's success through referrals, network contacts, advice, information, new business and support. The partners' task is to present an image which attracts and stimulates interest from a wide range of sources. This image must be such that it also promotes the firm's USP.

Phase 1 in Figure 7.1 illustrates that a positive image and a clear USP attract clients from the general public. When the firm provides excellent service, this positive image is reinforced for these clients. This leads to Phase 2 where these clients then recommend the firm to others so that the firm's image is further reinforced.

Alternatively, Phase 1 in Figure 7.2 shows the effects of a negative or unclear image and a lack of USP upon a firm's ability to attract new business. Those firms inevitably attract fewer clients. This situation is aggravated in Phase 2 if clients then have a negative experience of the firm. This, in turn, leads to even fewer, if any, referrals.

Unfortunately, negative experiences result as much from professionals' attitude and behaviour as from the service they provide. Partners need to discover how the firm is perceived by its different audiences. Aubrey Wilson proposes that there are four images which a professional firm best considers. These are:

- **the current image** how the firm is *actually* perceived
- **the mirror image** how the firm *imagines* it is perceived
- **the wish image** how the firm *would like* to be perceived

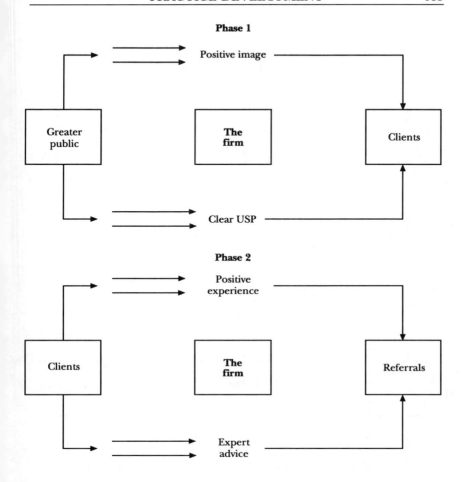

Figure 7.1   Positive image.

- **the optimum image** how the three images can be *aligned* to serve the firm.

The current image

Information about the public's perception of the firm is essential if partners wish to develop their practice. Anecdotal reassurance or a

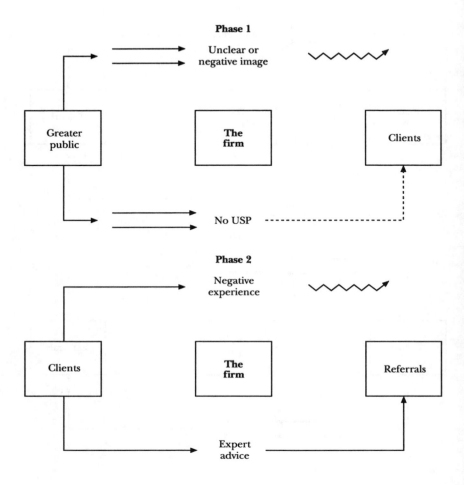

Figure 7.2 Negative image.

'best guess' approach has little value when assessing *current image* because it leads to repeated behaviour rather than change, development and an improved image. The firm's best source of information about current image is its own clients. These can be encouraged to give frank opinions when they are surveyed anonymously.

Surprisingly, many professionals argue that *their clients* have nothing to hide and do not need anonymity. Even so, a request for a serious and reflective response means that clients are free to disclose negative reactions as well as positive ones. They find this easier to do when they are assured that their remarks do not jeopardize their ongoing professional relationships. Anonymity for this reason is essential.

Asking clients to complete and then hand in a survey while seated in the firm's reception area is a temptation always to be resisted. This data collection method obviously limits an honest response because they can imagine their names being added to the survey just after they return it. The following survey sample provides a set of generic questions designed to gain information from clients about the firm. The items are easily adapted to meet the individual needs of different firms

---

Sample client survey

The following items are of use when surveying clients about their current perceptions of the firm.

1 Are you satisfied overall with the quality of your advisers' technical advice?

Yes   *No*   *Please comment*

2 Based on expertise alone, would you recommend your:

   • adviser without qualification?

Yes   *No*   *Please comment*

   • the firm without qualification?

Yes   *No*   *Please comment*

3 Do the fees charged represent value for money?

Yes   *No*   *Please comment*

---

4 During the last 12 months, how frequently did you request a service from the firm?

—   *Once*   —   *More than 4 times*
—   *2 to 4 times*   —   *Not at all*

5 Are practice hours convenient for you?

Yes   *No*   *Please comment*

6 How did you choose your adviser?

7 Are you aware of the firm's specialist areas?

Yes   *No*   *Please comment*

8 Please list the services which you know the firm provides.

9 Do you always meet with the same adviser? If not, please comment.

Yes   *No*   *Please comment*

10 Does your adviser listen to you?

Yes   *No*   *Please comment*

11 Can you understand your adviser's suggestions, comments and requests?

Yes   *No*   *Please comment*

12 Would you change firms if a different professional firm were highly recommended?

Yes   *No*   *Please comment*

13 What services offered by the practice do you find most valuable? (list the services here)

14 Do your advisers answer your phone calls, letters, requests?

Yes   *No*   *Please comment*

15 Do you find your adviser helpful?

   Yes   *No*   *Please comment*

16 Does your adviser keep you waiting?

   Yes   *No*   *Please comment*

17 Please score the following practice facilities:

	Poor	*Adequate*	*Good*
● reception			
cleanliness	—	—	—
comfort	—	—	—
relaxation	—	—	—
beauty	—	—	—
● parking	—	—	—
● facilities for the handicapped	—	—	—
● consultation			
privacy	—	—	—
seating	—	—	—
freedom from interruption	—	—	—

18 Please comment on the following support offered by the practice:

	Poor	*Adequate*	*Good*
● record-keeping	—	—	—
● reception staff			
telephone manner	—	—	—
discretion	—	—	—
helpfulness	—	—	—

Additional survey groups

Other groups in addition to clients should also be surveyed where this is feasible. The goal is to learn as much as possible about how the firm is generally perceived within the community. Another valuable source of information comes from the firm's own support staff. Partners who assume that the staff are admirers of their work should consider how much new business is developed as a result of staff members' referrals. If none, then partners should well ask why. Of course, if staff are surveyed, then it is particularly important that their anonymity be respected. As an added reassurance of this, it is a good idea to invite a disinterested outsider to hand out and then collect staff surveys. Questions posed to staff should also avoid requests for handwritten answers.

The mirror image

This refers to the way in which members of the firm *imagine* that the practice is perceived. Generally, this is a more flattering image than the one revealed through client surveys. Partners can complete the same survey they give to their clients and then compare results. Any differences between information collected about the firm's *current image* and the views expressed about its *mirror image* need immediate evaluation and action.

The wish image

The *wish image* refers to the way in which members of the firm *would like* it to be perceived. This is linked to partners' aspirations and their vision for the firm (see page 82). If partners agree to common values and priorities, then this contributes to the development of an ideal image for the firm. An ideal image encourages the pursuit of the firm's goals. This process is considerably aided if the firm has information about its current and mirror images upon which to base any strategy for change.

The optimum image

This refers to alignment of the three other images so that the firm gives a coherent and consistent message to the public. Clients who are attracted by this image are most likely to have a positive experience of the firm because the *optimum image* is based upon the conscious choices of firm members to give excellent client service.

CUSTOMER SERVICE

Client surveys are a valuable means for gaining information about practice image. They can also be designed to gather information about what services clients most want and need. With this information, partners can add those services which meet genuine client demand. Much is written about the importance of customer service, particularly in relation to Total Quality Management programmes (see page 37). The arguments in favour of a client-centred practice are very convincing. Even so, many practice leaders resist both quality and customer service programmes because their potential cost seems daunting in terms of time and money for evaluation, training and improvement of facilities. They are able to be more enthusiastic if they are shown that this investment directly enhances the firm or actually increases practice income.

Arthur D. Little, the international consultancy, has researched customer service and suggests that the resulting benefits from attention to customer satisfaction can actually be measured. The consultancy proposes that a firm, first, identifies what services clients value and need and then, second, meets these specific requirements. The resulting increased business is a measurable benefit. An adaptation of the Arthur D. Little approach essentially includes the following activities:

- identifying those services of vital importance to the client through surveys and interviews
- identifying the severity of client response when this service is not offered or is poorly executed
- determining how well this service is currently offered by the firm
- determining how well this service is currently offered by the firm's competitors
- identifying services which clients desire but do not seek from the firm: this includes clients' do-it-yourself efforts, their consulting non-professional advisers or competing firms.

The task is to discover the gaps between the services which clients want and those which they are currently offered by the firm. When customer service effort is directed toward filling this gap, then the increased demand for newly offered or improved services is a measurable benefit gained from this. The firm which benefits most from customer service is the one that identifies valued services and then offers them in a way that clients genuinely appreciate. This brings a strategic approach to customer service because the potential costs of development efforts are measurable as well as the potential benefits to the firm in terms of increased business.

A survey about customer service requirements has a different focus from that of the current image survey. Questions in the image survey seek information about how *the firm* is actually perceived. A client service survey asks clients to describe their *service ideals*, that is, what they really need and want in general. The latter survey is not primarily concerned with gathering information about a specific firm although some information-gathering items can be included. Its purpose is to identify service areas of value and importance to the client. Partners can then ask themselves whether their firm provides these services and, if not, whether it is possible and appropriate for the firm to develop them. A sample of items that could be included in this kind of client survey follows.

- It is important that my calls are returned within 24 hours.

  1   ⟵————————————————————⟶   10
  Low   *High*

- It is important that I receive regular reports on the status of my project.

  1   ⟵————————————————————⟶   10
  Low   *High*

- It is important that my professional advisers visit my office.

  1   ⟵————————————————————⟶   10
  Low   *High*

- It is important that I receive an early response to my requests for meetings.

1 ←————————————————————————————→ 10
Low   *High*

These are just a few of the possible items about service needs which could be included. This survey is an opportunity for partners to discover what clients think about a variety of service options and also patterns of professional behaviour. They can include items which refer to services they already offer as well as those which ask about potential services. The aim of this survey is to gather information about general preferences and client ideals.

To illustrate this, consider a firm of solicitors facing additional competition in their local area. One of the two new firms is a three-partner practice and the other is a new regional office of a London-based firm. The established partners feel secure in their ability to maintain their current client list and yet they are aware that new clients must always be added in order to offset natural client attrition. Their area is gradually changing so that its mixture of small store front businesses, private houses and light manufacturing is being replaced by a large shopping centre, a relocated utility firm and blocks of high-quality flats.

The partners in the established firm need to know if the kind of service they offer meets the needs of the new incoming population. To gain this information, they need to identify what services their present clients and the members of their gradually changing community actually want the most. Their traditional services include the provision of general legal advice, and the partners need to assess the way in which the firm delivers these services. This refers specifically to meetings, reports, letters, telephone contact, fees, billing information, and more, as well as to related issues, such as office facilities, hours of opening, staff behaviour and courtesy, timeliness of reports, response to deadlines, follow-up of client contact, communication skills and more.

Gathering information about client preferences and needs helps the partners stay in touch with shifts and changes in their community. If, for example, they discover that commuters from the luxury flats would appreciate evening appointments, their decision to offer this service potentially leads to a new source of clients. Other new additions to the community, such as the utility firm or the shopping centre businesses, are likely to value different services. Through a customer service survey, the partners can discover what these potential clients value and want.

If a new service initially seems to contradict the firm's long-term needs, it can be explored further to discover whether it can be adapted to match the firm's overall development strategy. With a flexible attitude, new insights into what clients want brings a fresh perspective to the partners' attitude to service provision.

PROBLEM – ANALYSIS – DISCUSSION

Problem

Five years ago, an association of dentists was formed by a group of independent dental practices. Their purpose was the provision of mutual support, shared training costs and the development of a strategy for promoting dental services throughout their area. The association grew rapidly from five to 33 member surgeries, and their quarterly conferences provided a forum for delegates to discuss development issues and learn about new initiatives in dental practice.

During one such conference, a delegate described a mail-order firm he saw in operation during a recent visit to Australia. This firm sold incentive goods to dental surgeries, and its products included greeting and appointment cards, relaxation music tapes, toys for children's play areas, specialized reception magazines, key rings and a variety of other novelty items. He showed his colleagues the company's well-presented brochures. Several delegates were so interested that they wanted to order the goods from him right away.

Instead, he proposed that their whole association assume a sales unit role and share any discounts among the members. After some discussion, the others convinced him to assume this role himself. Several very vocal members assured him that they definitely would order. Pleased that his idea was so warmly received, the dentist decided to go ahead and write to Australia for more information.

The mail-order firm answered immediately, explaining that they required sales representatives to act as independent business units. This meant that they paid in advance for goods and managed all sales themselves. There would also be a 'one-time franchise fee' that permitted the use of the mail-order company's name. After looking through the provided literature, the dentist realized that even minimum sales would supplement his present income very well.

He sent a cheque right away in payment of the franchise fee and for placement of a large order of attractive-looking items. Just after he mailed this, he also realized that he had just become an importer of goods. Although his solicitor took partial care of this, the dentist put a half-day of surgery time into organizing the necessary paperwork himself. He also used another day to prepare a short brochure to promote his product line.

Ten weeks later, a notice arrived telling him to pick up his goods at a Custom's Inspection Centre. After going through the required paperwork, an official gave him a battered and water-stained cardboard box. The goods inside bore only the slightest resemblance to the items presented in the brochure.

On return to his surgery, he phoned the Australian company. Only then did he learn that the firm whose goods he first saw in Australia had been taken over by the firm to which he had mailed his cheque. Also, the contract which he signed, without first showing his solicitor, required that he place at least two more substantial orders. The ultimate aggravation, though, was his discovery that all liability for goods damaged in transit belonged to him.

Analysis

1 In what ways is the mail-order idea potentially beneficial to the dentist's practice?

2 In terms of USP and customer service, in what ways is it a bad idea?

3 How could he have acted to gain the benefits and minimize the risks?

4   How would a customer service survey have helped him better develop this project?

Discussion

Although this problem describes difficulties associated with selling goods rather than services, it highlights essential development issues for professional firms. These include:

- Know colleagues thoroughly before going into any kind of joint venture
- Take care when offering a new product or service; a perceived demand often obscures difficulties
- Practice promotion, client care and new service ideas always require money and time. Potential expenses should be examined when deciding a development strategy. There are low-cost methods, but these require careful planning.

A main benefit from offering a mail-order service is the potential it brings the dentist for raising his profile within the profession. This leads to new contacts and experiences which further enhance his practice. Unfortunately, this dentist has undertaken the project without real awareness of the necessary investment. Particularly, because mail order is so very different from dental surgery, he should have carefully considered the vision he has for his practice and his long-term goals before taking any action. His new ideas would then be assessed in terms of their impact on his whole practice.

If he acknowledges that the idea means major change, this leads to recognition that he needs more time to research it. Surely, there are firms within his own country that sell incentive goods. A national supplier eases the start-up challenge considerably. While every feature of this project actually signals a *bad idea* its essential weakness is the dentist's impulsive behaviour. The decision to place an order resulted from an emotional reaction to his colleagues' show of support and a belief that he could make money quickly and easily. These two ingredients are a recipe for disaster.

Rather than react immediately to his colleagues' enthusiasm, the dentist should have surveyed a greater number of dentists, and then widened the audience to include dental hygienists, GPs and veterinary surgeons. A survey gives him a more specific idea of potential clients' needs and avoids selection of sales goods based upon his personal taste.

SUMMARY

This chapter emphasizes the importance of marketing the firm's services. It is proposed that the use of networks is a major trend in terms of practice promotion. The benefits of active networking are explained. A series of analysis questions focus on the development of a firm's Unique Selling Proposition or USP. This is defined as a practice strength which meets a client demand more effectively than does the competition. Practice image is discussed and it is emphasized that image is one area of practice development which a firm cannot avoid. A sample survey is offered to aid the discovery of how the firm is currently perceived. The benefits of enhanced client service are presented, and it is suggested that increased business can be directly linked to meeting client demands.

8

Communication

FROM THE IMPLICIT TO THE EXPLICIT

Two partners are travelling together to meet an important client. One looks up from the documents he is studying and asks, 'Did you get the fax?' His colleague answers, 'Yes, thank you for that information', to which the first responds, 'Well, what did you think?' After the second answers, 'Very helpful, thank you', they both return to reading their notes.

At a critical point during the meeting that follows, the client asks the two partners an important question. They answer simultaneously, and yet one says 'yes' and the other 'no.' After the meeting, the first partner asks his colleague, 'How could you do that, you said that you read the fax I sent you with background information on that point.' It is only then that they discover that they were each referring to different faxes. The moral of the story is this: It is tempting to assume a complete understanding of what someone else is saying, but this is as rare as it is unlikely. Assumptions about what other people mean are only guesses in disguise.

George Brown, Professor Emeritus at the University of California and internationally recognized Gestalt therapist, proposes that effective communication depends upon *awareness*, that is, individuals listen carefully to themselves when they speak and to others when they listen. They are interested in the way in which the message is delivered as well as its content. Awareness, as the term is used here, requires a robust commitment to creating understanding and a vigorous avoidance of guess work to ascertain meaning. This approach to communication ensures that there is mutual understanding because it is based on actually asking what the other person means when there is doubt, ambiguity or the possibility of error.

The dilemma is knowing when it is necessary to ask. All conversation could grind to a halt if every detail were double-checked for understanding. In general, those messages that are heavily laden with *implicit information* are those which potentially lead to miscommunication. Frequently this happens because an implicit message depends most on the guess work of the listener. Where there are guesses, there are the most mistakes. Because professionals take verbal short cuts and use technical language which is incomprehensible to even very intelligent clients, they frequently present the obscure rather than state the obvious. Professional communication often *suggests and implies* information rather than *explains and makes explicit.*

Clients appreciate their professional adviser's efforts to communicate in a clear and simple manner. Two guidelines contribute to the professional's ability to do this. They are: make the implicit explicit and state the obvious about all essential features of professional advice. These two suggestions are deceptively simple and are also extremely difficult to follow. Even so, it is suggested that the clarity which they provide underlies effective communication. All of the ideas presented in this chapter encourage professionals to make the implicit explicit and to state the obvious in an effort to dramatically improve communication.

COMMUNICATION AS A SOCIAL SKILL

In the professions, technical expertise is essential and yet professionals also need to demonstrate social skill when they communicate. Their livelihood depends upon their ability to inspire confidence, encourage their staff and peers and also make it easy, understandable and pleasant for clients to receive their advice and services. It is socially aware behaviour which contributes to building long-term relationships with these staff, peers, and clients. Communication is an intrinsic part of this process with the articulate and perceptive gaining great potential for success.

Those clients who are uneasy, frightened, in crisis or in pain gain confidence when their professional adviser behaves with sensitivity and a willingness to listen. Clients value self-assertion and forcefulness only when these traits are used on their own behalf. Professionals need the ability to manipulate *their own personalities* so that they adapt their behaviour to meet the changing needs of each situation.

Owen Hargie is a communication expert and academic at the University of Ulster. He suggests that there are recognizable features which contribute to socially skilled behaviour and, therefore, to communication effectiveness. An adaptation of his findings to meet the needs of a professional audience highlights five features for socially skilled behaviour. These features lead to behaviour which is:

- goal-directed
- coherent
- appropriate to the situation
- able to be learned, and
- controlled.

Professional performance at its best demonstrates all of these features and yet this achievement takes years of practice, trial and error and determination. A study of these five social skills offers a system for improving communication. Particularly, when partners assume responsibility for guiding the development of junior firm members, these criteria allow a systematic means for evaluating their performance. Each of these five features is described here.

Goal-directed behaviour

This occurs when individuals have a specific outcome in mind when they initiate an interaction with others. For example, a solicitor meets a client in order to gain information and so directs all of the discussion toward that end. Although the discussion may also touch upon other issues, the solicitor does not lose sight of the initial goal and considers the interaction a success only when the goal has been achieved.

Coherent behaviour

This occurs when individuals behave so that they make a single harmonious impression. For example, a medical consultant synchronizes the use of stethoscope, verbal instructions, listening skills and eye contact when examining a patient. This fluid performance gives an overall impression of concentration and skill and inspires confidence in the patient.

Appropriate to the situation

This occurs when individuals recognize the need to match their behaviour to the needs of the situation. For example, the accountant who reserves expressions of anger or dismay when discovering that a client has withheld vital and compromising information. This adviser then seeks to explain the repercussions of such action in a non-judgemental way as well as sets limits for his or her future involvement with this client.

Learned behaviour

This occurs when individuals through observation or direct teaching learn separate activities and then integrate them into a single, skilled response. For example, the architect who blends verbal and visual presentation styles in order to discover what the client needs and desires. This professional knows that the use of a variety of different methods to gain this information increases the likelihood of creating a satisfactory project. In another example, there is the trainee barrister who imitates the courtroom tactics of the case's leader. Through direct observation this trainee begins the process of creating a unique personal style of advocacy.

Controlled behaviour

This occurs when individuals have sufficient ability to time their behaviour and choose how to express themselves. For example, the psychologist who listens to the client for a prolonged period of time, only intervening when a comment or reaction offers the client the most benefit.

These five features provide a foundation for effective communication. Interactions between individuals or within groups are improved when they are in use. In the following case study, the profiled professional describes communication behaviour which she believes is important within her firm. She places special emphasis on the relationship between partners and staff and also addresses the need for frank and open discussion among partners. Her remarks indicate that she possesses a high degree of social skill. Following the case study, her attitude and actions are analysed in terms of the five features of socially skilled behaviour described above.

CASE STUDY: CHANTREY VELLACOTT CHARTERED ACCOUNTANTS

The purpose of this case study is to highlight the importance of social skills when managing a professional firm. The professional involved presents her style of creating a positive work atmosphere and emphasizes the need for information exchange and performance review, all of which are communication issues.

Christine Freshwater is Finance Partner at the London-based firm of Chantrey Vellacott Chartered Accountants. Although highly skilled in her full-time role of financial management, she also recognizes the importance of promoting good work relationships among the members of the practice, particularly between partners and staff. She says, 'Although partners work with people all of the time, they generally are not personnel people. I believe that they have to be because when partners are, they communicate well and they can motivate their staff.'

In Christine's view, 'Staff should want to come to work and be able to enjoy what they do. You can develop this by playing fair by staff: pay them a reasonable amount and set them a job for which they are capable. If they do not get it right, you explain why and talk them through it. As well, you give them new things to do so that they take on more responsibility.' Her goal is to encourage staff to take a real interest in the work of the firm as a whole.

When asked how she actually promotes this, she explains, 'You can create a bit of fun. On one occasion, I gave a new staff member a difficult target to reach in just three days. Everyone in the office laughed along with the staff member when I set it, but then he almost achieved it. He had decided to go after it and he's now *set himself* some very difficult targets. The banter is around hard work. I like to see happy faces when people are working. Creating this is by trial and error because there has to be a limit and a balance to joking in the office. When everyone understands the limitations, then you develop a happy team.'

In professional firms, atmosphere is important, particularly because non-professional staff have limited potential for career advancement. A positive work environment can encourage long-term commitment from staff so that the firm's professionals gain consistent and reliable back-up for serving clients. Even so, Christine also encourages training among staff. This creates a certain risk because their improved skills can lead them to leave the firm. She sees that this is highly acceptable because their increased proficiency makes them more interested in their job and more productive while they remain in the firm.

With the right calibre of people in place, Christine suggests that a practice also needs a system of communication which serves the whole of the firm. At Chantrey Vellacott, three communication areas are identified: inter-office between London and the firm's regional offices, inter-department within the London office, and database usage for client development. The partners hold a briefing meeting once per month (in addition to their twice-yearly formal partners' meeting). Each department within the London office and each regional office also holds monthly briefing meetings which allows circulation of information from the partners' briefing.

Christine explains the rationale for briefing staff and non-partner professionals on practice issues. 'When people report to a partner or manager, they should have adequate explanations for any limitations or requirements. Well-trained and well-briefed staff feel they are part of a team and then they pull in the same direction as you.'

Staff depend on partners for information about the firm's priorities and initiatives. They also want to know their work requirements and how they are assessed. This information allows them to contribute more to their work. Christine says, 'Partners shouldn't resent the time it takes to inform staff. In many firms, though, they often do. This could be a result of the way that some firms are organized, where partners all receive the same profit-share regardless of hours, quality of work, new business or their behaviour within the firm.'

She suggests that this system is based on the assumption that everyone knows their work and that they simply do it. 'This could explain why partners treat staff the way that they do. There is a great expectation that people will just get on and do the obvious thing. This does not work. You have to ask people to achieve certain performance levels and then explain exactly what you want. This helps to motivate people.'

This leads Christine to reflect on the value of direct feedback and performance review for all members of a firm, including the partners: 'Being a partner is just a title. You may have achieved it for technical reasons, client development or for other reasons. There are a range of backgrounds, skills and personalities among partners and yet there is this general idea that partners automatically know how to perform at their best.

'I firmly believe that partners should sit down annually and discuss their objectives, hopes and aspirations. This is an opportunity to help people focus on development. We're all capable of improvement. There should be a mechanism in place that guides everyone within the firm to develop their full potential.' Such a commitment to improved performance impacts technical skills as well as social skills of communication.

AN ANALYSIS OF SOCIAL SKILLS

In this case study, Christine proposes that staff should have a positive atmosphere in which to work. She believes that this leads to improved performance. When she shares a joke, listens to staff or takes time to explain partner-level decisions, this directly supports her goals of creating a positive atmosphere and encouraging high standards of performance. In person, her manner is humour-filled and yet this is balanced by an impression of underlying seriousness. Overall, she presents a highly credible and coherent image particularly when she describes the need for a pleasant office atmosphere and also criteria for practice excellence.

Long experience in leadership positions allows her to trust her own judgement when encouraging appropriate behaviour within the firm. As Finance Partner she has considerable authority and she seems very natural in this role. In fact, she has learned how to lead through a progression of management roles and by acquiring numerous separate skills. These include ongoing development of her technical expertise, decision making skills, personnel technique, confident presentation and an ability to articulate objectives clearly, among other skills.

While being interviewed for this case, circumstances required that she change roles at least three times: from high level practice leader to supportive guide of junior staff to relaxed social contact. Her adaptation from role to role as she addressed each situation was highly disciplined so that her communication performance was seamless. All of this indicates that this professional has social skills.

MESSAGES: SENT AND RECEIVED

Communication means that an exchange of messages is taking place. These messages can be verbal or non-verbal, and only require that there is at least one sender and one receiver. When communication occurs between socially skilled individuals, there is an increased likelihood that clear, accurate and meaningful messages are exchanged and that misunderstandings are likely to be corrected with least upset when they do occur. Alternatively, when communication is based upon an assumption of understanding, then virtually anything can happen.

Consider making a routine request to an office clerk for a client file. Seemingly, the only requirement for successful communication is the provision of a name or a number for the file. Even so, this simple request is executed using a variety of methods, such as, audio tape, electronic mail, telephone, face to face contact or a written memo, and mistakes can easily occur at this initial stage. Later, misunderstandings potentially arise about urgency, format needs (diskette, computer screen or paper copies) and place of delivery, among many other problems. As messages become more complicated, the potential for serious mishap increases in relation to this complexity.

'Rich' communication

Professional communication is both complex and specialized. Therefore any exchange between a trained professional and a lay client is fraught with potential misunderstanding. Researchers and theorists identify three available levels of communication. These are:

- **written**   In English, this includes the use of 29 symbols (26 letters and 3 punctuation marks).
- **vocal**   In English, there are 32 symbol phonemes (sounds) with variations provided by pitch, accent, pause and intonation.
- **visual and**   This includes all of the vocal variations as well
  vocal   as gestures, eye contact, and bodily positions.

When a message is important, or there is any potential for mistakes, then it is advisable to use a method of communication that allows face-to-face contact. This level of communication provides maximum opportunity to express subtle and complex messages because there are a variety of vocal and visual symbols available. It allows the speaker to convey *richness* of meaning. The term richness is used by communication experts to refer to the depth and breadth of meaning presented through a message. They suggest that it is highly beneficial to meet face to face when dealing with difficult situations.

Because written communication provides least opportunity for expressing subtle meaning, it is best avoided when subtlety and nuance are required in communication. Written communication is most useful and necessary when:

- there is a great deal of information
- accuracy and detail are crucial
- many people receive the same message
- a record or history of contact must be established
- the message goes beyond the initial recipient.

Voice-to-voice contact over the telephone offers a compromise between face-to-face and written communication. Technological advances in recent years have added the possibility of televiewing with video telephone conversations. As this service improves, it increases the 'richness' of voice-to-voice communication, but cannot substitute for actual face-to-face meetings. Physical presence communicates subtle information about the speaker as well as the content of the message being presented.

Paying attention

Although senders of information focus primarily on encoding a message and then transmitting it, they also need to consider how their message is being received. Social skills are of particular value here because the emphasis is on developing awareness about what is occurring between message senders and receivers. When socially skilled communicators send a message, they are aware that its accurate reception is essential. These communicators always pay attention to the comprehension of their listeners. This is as important to them as the message itself.

Goal-orientated communication such as this is effective because the sender has criteria for a successful exchange. Goals encourage speakers to pay close attention to their audience in order to discover if their message is understood. Communication is only complete for these speakers when their goal is achieved. Therefore, they are willing to alter their message and style of delivery until this happens. Ultimately, having goals for communication creates a flexible presentation style because speakers adapt to the needs of their audience.

For example, the end-goal for narration of a joke is spontaneous laughter. While telling the joke, the speaker watches to see if the listener grasps the meaning of the joke and is highly sensitive to the way in which the joke is received. The desire to raise a laugh occasionally requires the narrator to amplify the story, modify vocal delivery, and change body language as necessary. The communication is only considered a success when the joke is finally understood and the audience laughs.

Alternatively, there are speakers who are immune to any and all signals from their audience of disinterest, boredom, anger or even despair. Their presentations roll on regardless of audience response. If these speakers set specific goals for communication, then they would unavoidably lift themselves out of their routine performance. To be a bore to friends, clients or colleagues is an unlikely goal for even the most self-centred professional. When listeners' reactions are given importance and are also observed, then speakers improve their performance. Goals do not ensure successful communication, but they do provide criteria for measuring success.

Each of the other four features for socially skilled behaviour also contribute to communication effectiveness. The following analysis questions serve professionals who recognize the need for planning important interactions. Considering social skill issues in advance leads to communication that is efficient, directed and effective.

Analysis 10

This analysis guides preparation for important interactions.

1   What purpose should this interaction serve:

- personally
- professionally?

2   How will I know when the purpose is achieved?

3   What effort can I make to coordinate my appearance, words and actions so that I make a single harmonious impression?

4   How can I best match my behaviour to the situation's needs?

5   What different actions, aids or behaviour will best get my message across?

6   What past experience can I draw upon to guide preparation for this interaction?

7   Are there any professional limits to sharing information or a need to pace the interaction or time my comments?

If a client has expressed dissatisfaction with the firm's service or one of its professionals, communication with that client needs diagnosis. Social skill criteria provide a foundation for analysis of communication breakdown or serious misunderstanding. The following questions focus on specific elements of a past interaction toward understanding the sources of any negative reactions.

Analysis 11
This analysis guides diagnosis of past interactions.

1   What was my purpose for this interaction:

   ● personal
   ● professional?

2   How did I plan to judge that my purpose was achieved?

3   Was there anything about my behaviour which created an uncoordinated impression:

   ● dress   ● gender
   ● eye contact   ● gestures
   ● language   ● technical expertise
   ● age

4   How did I identify the situation's needs during this interaction?

5   How well did I adapt my behaviour to the situation?

6   Did I pace my behaviour so that the other person could understand what I was saying?

7   Did the listener indicate that I provided depth of information?

8   What past experiences were similar to this occasion? Is there any history or pattern of problems with this kind of situation?

Overcoming bias

In Chapter 5 (see page 142), the impact of language on decision making is discussed, with particular reference to the bias caused by a speaker's choice of words. There are other kinds of bias which also have a powerful effect on a listener's ability to hear and interpret accurately what is said. These biases are: selling, filters and unfinished business.

Selling

Experienced professionals generally make a conscious effort to over-come any obvious sources of bias. They acquire this skill through daily dealings with colleagues and clients from very different backgrounds. Unfortunately, some forms of bias work at a perceptual or unconscious level so that reactions to an idea, event or person occur without the professional's awareness. This kind of perceptual influence is widely used by advertisers who know which colours, words and images sell their products best. Their task is to convince a consumer to buy without revealing the extent of their powers of persuasion.

When a socially skilled speaker knows how to 'sell' a message, then listeners benefit, assuming that they are not the subject of fraud. Clear and well-formulated messages are received with less effort than confused and rambling ones. An articulate presenter can use style to create a bias which favours a message. Although social skills are requirements for effective communication, they also add distortion to a message by creating a positive impression on the listener. Alternatively, when listeners are annoyed by a speaker's delivery, this turns them off to further listening.

Professionals benefit when they recognize their ability to influence as well as to be influenced. This refers to both obvious and conscious ways as well as subtle and unconscious ones. Although there is complete justification in having a negative reaction to a poor or ill-prepared speaker, a project's success often depends upon making sense of information from a variety of sources. It is counter-productive to allow bias to curtail listening to poor presenters. In contrast, a natural willingness to listen to an articulate speaker can also influence proceedings. An inspired presenter, as any barrister can attest, lends credibility to even the weakest ideas. Discovering or admitting to both positive and negative bias is a source of strength for professionals.

Filters

A filter refers to the way in which people habitually interpret information and their own experiences. People develop a mental routine during the course of their lives so that they automatically ignore some kinds of information or focus their attention on others. Filtering is a form of bias and there are as many kinds of filters as there are human beings.

This explains at least in part why two partners can attend the same meeting and later describe what occurred in contradictory terms. The same events play out before them both but their perceptions of the events are different. They need to recognize how, why and when they filtered the experience. This allows them to counteract this tendency on other occasions and, therefore, listen more effectively.

Certain kinds of events, people and situations lend themselves to filtering more than others. It is ironic that the existence of a filter impedes the discovery of its source. The following sections highlight four influences which frequently contribute to the filtering of information. Each of these topics includes analysis questions.

The credibility of the source

Ideas 'borrow' credibility from their source. Presenters' past history, their standing within a firm or their social status influences the way in which their comments are received. If the acceptance or rejection of information is based upon insubstantial criteria, then this is to the detriment of the firm.

- *Key question:*
  Does the speaker's style, credentials or experience inspire confidence or invite acceptance of what is said?

  If yes, then ask if the speaker's status casts an overly positive light on the presented information.

If no, then ask if the speaker's status casts a negative light on the presentation's ideas because their validity is automatically questioned.

Common background

Professionals who value most the ideas of colleagues from similar backgrounds limit their capacity to absorb new points of view. They 'hear' only that information which reinforces what they already know. This inevitably endangers the firm.

- *Key question*

  Does the speaker share a common background or set of experiences with the listener?

  If yes, then question *any* assumptions of a shared agreement for ideas, values and beliefs. Explore potential differences in order to create more realistic agreement.

  If no, then explore the potential existence of *less obvious* shared ideas, values and beliefs. Having sought common ground first, then decide if the speaker can, after all, understand and address common interests.

Information overload

There is so much information generated through new technology that separate sets of skills have evolved for gathering, studying and understanding it. Excessive amounts of information can actually hinder productivity. The risk in this case is the loss of vital information and inaccurate comprehension. Information overload causes listeners to absorb only that information which already makes sense to them or which fits into their preconceived ideas.

- *Key question*

  Is information presented so rapidly and extensively that it cannot be assimilated or understood?

In response, the flow can best be controlled when the source is technological. When the source is human, then social skills must be used to manage the situation. In either case, use of forms and requests for single-page summaries at designated intervals help minimize this perceptual problem.

Attractiveness of the presenter

This requires assessing the impact of friendship, emotional comfort and feelings of goodwill. Because these issues are usually seen in a positive light, listeners are less willing to limit their influence.

- *Key question*
  Does the listener feel drawn to the speaker as a result of charm, physical traits or for other personal reasons?

  If yes, then ask if this leads to excluding any negative or unpleasant information.

  If no, then ask if any positive or beneficial messages are likely to be excluded.

This last item is subtle and causes a great deal of filtering. Even if feelings of attraction (or repulsion) are acknowledged, it is extremely difficult to see through this bias and change behaviour. When attractive and credible speakers deliver information clearly and concisely, there is most need for good judgement, intelligence and individual experience to determine the influence of positive bias.

Unfinished business

When clients or colleagues feel anxious, confused or upset, they are often unable to listen. They bring *unfinished business* to the conversation. Even the most articulate and socially skilled speaker cannot get through to people who are thinking about something else. Professionals need a number of techniques at their disposal to make contact with distracted clients and colleagues. The ability to encourage attentive listening in highly charged or emotional situations is a valuable skill. Advisers who deal successfully with unfinished business so that clients gain benefit from what is said, create very strong client to professional relationships.

The main difficulty is discovering when clients and colleagues are not listening. They are not likely to admit this because it is a behaviour generally considered to be rude. As well, confronting people or questioning them closely about whether they are listening is rarely prudent. Any behaviour resembling that of a teacher in the classroom is not appreciated, particularly by clients. Instead, professionals need to pay attention to the clients' voice tone and its volume, the amount of eye contact, and the frequency and quality of their responding remarks.

When convening an important meeting, professionals should assess the degree of openness or ability to listen of those seeking professional advice. This allows them to adjust their presentation style to match their clients' needs. Distracted clients need to have key points repeated to them. This is unavoidable if the adviser is committed to their clients' gaining a full understanding. The following suggestions provide a means to do this without confrontation.

- At the outset of a meeting or conversation, ask, 'Is there anything you wish to discuss from our last [form of contact]?' And then *pause* to give the person time to answer the question. The vocal quality of their answer reveals valuable information about their state of mind. For example, a firm, strong 'no' is an obvious signal that the person is fully 'present'. A soft or half-swallowed answer from a normally forthright person is a signal that they have unfinished business, either with the adviser or from an unrelated situation. Even if they say, 'Carry on', the professional should be prepared for less than high-quality listening.
- If unfinished business is suspected, the professional should ask a follow-up question such as, 'Is there anything further that I should know before we continue?' Again, it is the quality of the response which provides valuable information.

  Another step to resolve inattention is to ask the client to join in making a summary of key points at intervals. This leads to the person absorbing information in small units so that better comprehension is ensured. To encourage this, the professional says, 'Let's highlight some of the major points. What stands out for you?'

- If this remark or another with a similar purpose fails to gain the person's attention, then the professional should assume there is a serious cause for inattention. Unfinished business can result from a variety of sources including: from personal issues arising from outside the meeting, fear of the unknown, shock or even unspoken dissatisfaction with the professional's service.

  If every effort to gain full attention fails, it is best to say gently, but directly, 'I have the impression that you are not taking in all of this information. If I am right, is there any distraction that you would like to discuss?' Next, allow a long pause for the question to make an impression. This pause also gives the client time to organize thoughts and comments. It is counter-productive to ask a question and then immediately carry on talking. At best the professional seems insensitive and, at worst, insincere.

- If the client discloses problems unrelated to the firm's work, it is appropriate to suggest that the person seek additional professional advice. The firm can have a list of recognized referral agencies available for this kind of situation. This is a courtesy service for the client who is likely to reward their advisers with loyalty and references to others about the firm's willingness to take a personal interest. The indirect benefits of listening are immense.

CONTACT INSIDE THE FIRM

Although it is essential that the successful firm employs articulate people, it also needs well-designed systems for both its internal and external communication. This ensures that it has a consistent, efficient and effective means for transmitting information. Its internal communication system provides links within the firm so that information circulates freely and members of the practice learn about all of the firm's activities. Its external system maintains contact with clients, regulatory bodies, professional organizations and is the firm's primary means for integrating into the community.

In some organizations, the communication system is unplanned. As the firm grows and activities become more complex, it unintentionally adopts procedures. Once begun, habits of making contact with one another inside the firm then become a routine so that gradually this becomes the firm's internal communication system. In a similar way, the partner's behaviour when using the telephone, writing letters or reports and leading meetings gradually forms a communication system for managing outside contacts. Ideally, a communication system is based on a plan and is also regularly evaluated for effectiveness.

Using networks

Networks are discussed in Chapter 7 (see page 176), in reference to developing contacts with outside groups. This idea also applies to communication inside the firm where a network is another name for the channel through which information is exchanged. All of the individual members of a practice form part of a larger group, and together they form a network of contacts and shared associations. Some contacts are fleeting. For example, trainee professionals develop skills and then often move into more permanent positions within the firm. Their expanding number of contacts as they assume each new position is their own network. Every organization contains this kind of informal network as well as those officially acknowledged by management.

If the partners wish to improve the firm's internal communication system, they need first to explore how its current system works. This includes the need to examine each of its networks: formal and informal. There are four different networks which typically exist in every organization, regardless of business or size. These networks are either formal and recognized by the firm's leaders, or informal and exist as a more casual aspect of everyday communication. Wise leaders work with networks never against them. Three relevant issues concerning the development of communication networks are:

- how does information circulate within the firm?
- how much information control do partners believe they have?
- how much do they actually have?

There are four communication networks which are readily identified in most organizations. These are as follows.

- **Hierarchy** This network is related to the official roles and titles held by members of the firm. It requires users to follow set procedures in order to communicate official information and is highly formal. Its success depends entirely on the degree of commitment to information sharing within the firm. When there are holes or gaps in this network, then overall communication within the practice is seriously impaired.
- **Expert** This network serves the specialists and skilled people working within the firm. They are likely to be clustered into departments, divisions or projects. This network sends information to all metallurgists, all information managers or all property solicitors, regardless of their official positions in the hierarchy. This network provides back-up to the hierarchical network. It offers a direct link from the management to the firm's specialist groups. Encouraging communication across specialist areas is a powerful means for team building within the firm.
- **Influential** This network includes those who have prestige and power within the firm, whether through politics, seniority, skills and talents, family or personal relationships or charisma. It offers an informal means of communication which results directly from these personal contacts. Members of this network do not necessarily have designated leadership roles, rather, their influence results from colleagues' seeking to make contact with them. Practice leaders should know who has this kind of influence and encourage them to work within the official communication system. They are unlikely to give up their informal methods and yet can be convinced to use the firm's formal system.
- **Friendship** This network is composed of personal friends, family and well-wishers within the firm. Its use requires providing and seeking information that serves individual needs. It is the most

informal of the networks. When it is used by senior members of a firm to advance their friends and family, it is often called nepotism. It is also the source of cliques and splinter groups. The task is to have a balanced atmosphere within the firm so that friends are comfortable together and yet do not exclude others from full participation in business activities.

'The grapevine' within companies is primarily made up of contacts described here as 'Influence' and 'Friendship' networks. Expert networks also contribute to the grapevine because the practice of their specialisms often creates friendship and comraderie. In some firms, there are more partners than there are staff and associates. Informal communication among partners about professional matters is essential to the creation of an atmosphere of cooperation and team effort.

Research findings indicate that professionals prefer to have short and informal exchanges about business issues rather than long and formal meetings. It is also suggested that the frequency of professional exchange among colleagues has a direct and positive impact upon their productivity. Improved performance emerges naturally from regular and informal communication within and across departments.

Designing a system

Much is written about Japanese productivity, and occasionally, management theorists explain Japan's industrial success by referring to the style of management prevalent in that country. However, when this approach is copied by Western businesses, managers find that it often does not transfer well. At least some of this failure results from an attempt to copy a management style and yet ignore the Japanese approach to communication that supports it.

The Japanese are highly social people and freely use both informal and formal methods of communication to manage their business affairs. Their particular management approach works because it is supported by a very high commitment to sharing information. For example, Japanese leaders depend upon the grapevine as an appropriate means to transmit information throughout the firm. In contrast, the grapevine in the West is highly informal and merely tolerated by a firm's leaders.

In Japan, every level of employee openly uses the grapevine. Although it is also considered to be an informal communication method in Japan, it is 'institutionalized' in the sense that management recognizes it as an effective system for communication. This allows Japanese firms to maintain a flat organizational structure (see page 122) without fragmentation or widespread misunderstandings. Because information is provided through formal and informal methods, employees rapidly learn, not only facts about decisions, but also the human stories behind these decisions.

In contrast, Western businesses tend to depend upon formal communication. This approach serves the tall and thin organizational structure which more typically occurs in the West (see page 122). Leaders of professional firms should, first, decide how to organize their firm and, second, consider how to design a communication system so that it serves all of their organizational needs. The following analysis questions contribute to evaluating the firm's communication system.

Analysis 12

This activity is best completed using two marker pens of different colours.

1   Draw an outline of your firm's organizational system, showing the number of levels from the top to the bottom of the firm.

2   With a coloured marker, trace the *ideal flow* of information from the top to the bottom.

3   Using the other coloured marker, trace the *actual flow* of information from the top to the bottom. Highlight where you know or suspect blocks occur.

4   Does the firm have a system for non-partners and staff to offer their comments, suggestions and responses to the partners about their decisions? If so, please describe this.

5   From the point of view of the least powerful member of the firm, describe the system for offering money-saving ideas, business suggestions or warnings to those with most power.

6   List any weaknesses within the firm's communication system and refer to Chapter 4 (see page 92) in order to set planning objectives to improve them.

Geography

Physical location influences communication habits. There is ample research which shows that distance, physical barriers, stairs and lifts all have an impact on communication. People tend to maintain regular patterns at work: they use the same hallways, stairs and meeting areas as part of their daily routine. Their communication habits develop as part of this routine and in accordance with their physical location, activities and habitual movements. When major change occurs in a work environment, then work-related communication patterns change as well. One study suggests that within four months of a move, professionals change their long-term relationships with professional colleagues by 46 per cent. They begin to refer *primarily* to those geographically closest to them even if there had been no professional communication before or any history of shared expertise.

This is relevant information for practice leaders who are considering office refurbishment, building expansion or consolidation of offices. When deciding allocation of work space, they can encourage new relationships and work-related exchanges by placing unacquainted professionals together. They can also make collaboration easier by organizing space so that teams stay together.

A common error in organizing work space for professionals is to isolate them in cubicles or offices to allow concentrated work. This leads to a minimum allotment of space for communal meeting or gathering areas. This approach is often *in direct response to requests* from the professionals themselves. Current research indicates, though, that professionals' productivity increases when there are opportunities for regular *but* informal information exchanges among themselves. This is aided by the provision of a common room, open meeting lounges or seating areas to complement professionals' private cubicles.

Walls, floors, ceilings and furniture placement all provide leaders with the means to communicate subtle messages about company priorities. In an aerospace research laboratory in California, one newly appointed senior manager decided that his team needed additional work space so that they could expand their activities. Rather than deal with the politics of space allocation and the eventual disruption of moving the team, he requested a much-needed paint and refurbishment project for the entire floor which was the working space for three other divisions plus his own.

His proposal suggested that each area be painted in slightly different shades of the same colours. The three other senior managers who shared the floor with his division, considered themselves far too busy to get involved in such a trivial pursuit. Therefore, they left all decorating decisions to him. The work was completed over a long holiday weekend under the direct supervision of the new manager. When everyone next arrived at work, they automatically returned to their former work areas now designated by pleasant colour shadings. It took most of the day for these preoccupied and busy professionals to realize that each research division had 'lost' several square metres of work space to the new manager's area. His plan had consciously used colour, light and furnishings to expand his own domain by a very sizeable amount.

Those who work in open-plan offices benefit from considering how to communicate boundaries, privacy needs and availability to colleagues. Even where there is a requirement for uniformity across the office floor, small plants and placement of allocated furniture give non-verbal messages to colleagues. For example, a new travel path developed in front of one professional's desk after a major office-wide refurbishment. Colleagues seemed almost compelled to greet her as they passed. She finally stopped the interruptions by placing her 'assigned extra chair' and small table in the middle of the newly forming traffic path. This provided an invisible but effective barrier to unwanted communication from colleagues who then left her entirely in peace.

CONTACT OUTSIDE THE FIRM

Articulate members of the firm with excellent listening skills are valuable assets. To support their efforts, these professionals need a system for external communication. Issues to be addressed for effective external communication include: record-keeping, report and letter writing, telephone and meeting etiquette, follow-up contact and others.

Many professionals have their own idiosyncratic style for carrying on communication outside of the firm. Over time, they gradually develop their own methods for contacting clients, professionals from other firms and other disciplines, government agencies and professional societies. This is natural and normal.

Commitment to clients

It follows that in many firms, these professionals also use an individual style in their correspondence and personal presentation. This individualistic approach can and does coexist easily with communication standards which also ensure that clients have consistent and reliable contact with the firm. Although the communication requirements of each profession differ, the process of setting standards applies equally to them all.

First, partners should establish general categories of client contact. For example, these could include:

- meetings: the firm's office
- meetings: the client's office
- letters
- field work: (from law courts to land sites to hospitals
- reports
- billing procedures
- records
- telephone.

Each category can then lead to a discussion of the strengths and weaknesses of *what partners already do*. What they *ought to do* or *what works in other firms* should be disregarded; they should focus instead on real life and current behaviour. The first step is to identify the firm's present communication style before considering what, if anything, should change. A summary of this best includes individual and idiosyncratic behaviour and radically different styles among the partners.

For example, if partners in general behave in a casual manner, this can be an asset to those clients who feel comfortable with this. Practice leaders should be aware of this even if they see their task as improving communication by tightening controls. If they decide that the casual approach is best maintained, then all of the features of that approach are retained. However, partners need also to set minimum standards for client communication and add procedures which ensure that the partners and others follow them. Reliable and consistent communication can be carried out even as the firm also retains its casual style.

Specifically, poor telephone follow-up is a common complaint among clients. There are measures which bring control to telephone contact without changing or impairing the firm's current style of working with clients. These would include:

- accurate logs kept of numbers dialled and of calls received
- a policy of returning calls within a specified span of time
- standardized forms for message taking
- a policy to follow up decision-making calls with written confirmation.

These are among many solutions which partners can explore to improve external communication with the telephone. A professional approach to communication can only enhance a firm's overall image regardless of the styles of its individual members.

PROBLEM – ANALYSIS – DISCUSSION

Problem

During 45 years within the same pharmaceuticals company, the divisional director of research has been directly responsible for 65 per cent of its patent applications and, therefore, indirectly responsible for more than 50 per cent of the firm's current annual revenue. His commitment to research science is legendary and company executives have traditionally given him an enormous discretionary budget, complete control of scientific personnel issues and also of administration within his division.

For the last five years, this director has supervised a special team for development of a drug to treat a disease widespread in undeveloped countries. His initial interest in this project emerged when he visited Western Africa as a distinguished guest of an international health organization. Although he has never been motivated by commercial concerns, he has a natural instinct for business.

He is fully aware that successful, cost-effective treatment of this disease would immensely enhance the pharmaceutical company's international image as well as create a new market within the Third World. There would be subsidized payments for drugs to treat the illness coming from world relief organizations and governmental aid. Even so, these commercial issues do not interest him, and he does not refer to the drug's potential financial benefit in any of his communications to company executives.

His special team conducts their research in absolute secrecy to protect their findings from competition. Each year their expenses for this project increase significantly so that in the budget for year five, 25 per cent of the division's total research funds is dedicated to it. The director is satisfied because he believes that the team has made a major breakthrough and is likely to present their successful results during the next year.

In keeping with the research division's tradition, he has given company executives very little information. Formerly, these executives were content to allow the research division to get on with their work and simply filed away his single-page progress reports written 'in science language'. This year, the managing director is newly recruited from a major international pharmaceutical firm. He has a reputation for cutting costs and increasing revenue. Most of his experience in the industry has been in production and he has a healthy disrespect for ivory tower research scientists. The managing director learned 'the hard way' that if researchers are given too much freedom, they waste the company's money.

Surprisingly, he does not recognize how much the firm has

depended upon the current research director's efforts. They met only once socially and the research director has sent 'apologies for absence' to all five of the monthly executive meetings which the managing director has called since assuming his post. Therefore, when the research division's proposed annual budget reaches him for preliminary approval, he is shocked by the figures. He sees the enormous expense involved in the development of a drug that he believes could never pay for itself in future sales, *and worse*, there is no supporting information describing the project's progress.

Without hesitation, he writes a tersely worded memo to the research director saying that he requires a revised budget proposal which cuts funding for the new project by 75 per cent and which itemizes all expenses in detail. He believes that this measure not only asserts his authority but also sends a much-needed message of fiscal responsibility to the research division. When this memo reaches the research director, he laughs and then hesitates for just a moment before phoning his old friend, the chairman of the company's board.

Analysis

Please assume the role of a consultant advising the chairman of the board to resolve the communication problems between the company's managing director and its research director.

1 What social skills do each of these leaders need to develop?

2 How has bias interrupted communication between these two company leaders?

3 Is it wise for the managing director to write memos when he is angry? If not, what are his alternatives?

4 Is it appropriate for the research director to contact the chairman before seeking to resolve difficulties directly with the managing director himself? If not, what are his alternatives?

5 How can the communication system between the senior company executives and the research division be improved?

Discussion

Both leaders need to improve their social skills. Even though the research director has enough influential power to avoid changing his style, he should be encouraged to do so because it is better for the company overall. He has been in the company for 45 years and has a wealth of experience and wisdom to be passed on to a new generation of executives. His 'speaking in science' creates a handicap for their understanding him. He needs to be encouraged to extend his goals for communication to include the interests and needs of those responsible for running the business side of the company. Although his cooperation in this is unlikely, at least the attempt should be made.

The managing director needs to recognize the existence of authority and status other than his own. His behaviour has been highly inappropriate. This is possibly the result of experiencing only one kind of research scientist and therefore, basing all of his future actions on that model. He must now learn to behave differently because the scientist with whom he deals has far more *informal* power than he has himself. He needs also to develop more self-control. Sending memos in the heat of the moment is emotionally satisfying and yet extremely unwise.

Bias is driving both leaders' behaviour. The research director has chosen not to attend even one executive meeting and is largely unconcerned about company management issues. He assumes, though, that he will always be able to use his influence. This is unrealistic because influence flourishes only when individuals nourish new contacts as well as maintain former ones. He is also blinding himself to the financial realities of the company. A research laboratory is far removed from customer lawsuits, world recession or changes in the government's testing regulations. He needs to support the managing director in order to ensure that the firm stays viable.

The managing director perceives researchers as threats to the firm rather than its source of success. On the first occasion that the research director failed to attend his executive meeting, he should have personally visited the research laboratory to recap the meeting for him and ask for his advice and input. His main task is to harness the collective power of current company leaders. He cannot do this if he retreats behind the ceremony of meetings to communicate with them.

Both leaders must change their communication habits. They should reach an agreement about a method which works for them both and then honour that. Also, the research director should be discouraged from calling the chairman before discussing an issue thoroughly with the managing director. Otherwise, the chairman condones poor communication and contributes to bad feeling. This can be addressed by analysing the company's communication system. There is something seriously amiss when the managing director genuinely does not recognize the prestige of his colleague in research. Also, it is a sign of trouble that the only forum for exchange between research and executive areas is a monthly meeting. A system for information exchange should be developed based upon the company's current organization.

SUMMARY

This chapter suggests that improved communication begins with professionals developing greater personal awareness about their own communication behaviour. They are encouraged to examine five features of socially skilled behaviour to aid this process. 'Rich' communication is explained and a means for diagnosing three different kinds of bias is proposed. The communication needs inside the firm are addressed, including developing internal networks, designing a communication system which matches the firm's management structure and the impact of internal geography. Communication issues between the firm and its outside contacts are discussed.

9

Information management

A VITAL ASSET

Even ten years ago, a successful firm would have regarded the maintenance of its practice files and records as mainly routine administrative work. Now, developments in information technology (IT) have transformed this task beyond recognition. Professionals have access to vast amounts of knowledge and information from sources world-wide through telephone links and alternative electronic channels. This changes forever the way in which information is stored, retrieved, analysed and sent and makes preparation for the twenty-first century extremely difficult. The challenge is to work with current technology so that it paves the way for further innovation.

A computer system is only as strong as its developers are wise and perceptive. Frequently, errors in human judgement about technology requirements are presented as if they are problems with equipment and software so that little learning is gained from poorly planned computer investments. The challenge for partners is to make clear decisions about practice priorities and only then make selections to meet the firm's technology needs.

This situation is best illustrated by firms which attempt to create 'paper-free' electronic offices without also addressing human and political workplace realities. Success depends upon the people who work with the new systems to have an understanding of them. Even so, staff who are asked to work within paper-free environments may initially lack confidence in this system. As a result they may make paper back-up copies covertly 'just in case'. This behaviour frustrates those managers who have failed to explain sufficiently how back-up is provided electronically.

In 1992, the UK's Institute of Internal Auditors (see Appendix I for this address) published *Systems Auditability and Control (SAC)*. This is a reference work for auditors and offers a comprehensive analysis of risks and *best practice* for control of information technology. It is based on employee surveys from 400 leading companies world-wide. This edition supersedes the 1977 *SAC* report which became the standard reference for computer auditors.

The 1992 report highlights that 40 per cent of IT systems fail to meet business requirements and only 11 per cent execute proper control while systems are being developed and put into operation. These are management problems, not technology issues. Far-sighted decision making is required if expensive computer systems are to give the firm maximum benefit. The information power which the new technology offers professional firms needs as much careful management as the firm's finances. It is the task of the firm's top leaders to develop plans for long-term growth so that a match can be made between these needs and information technology.

CASE STUDY: BRITISH POSTGRADUATE MEDICAL FEDERATION

The purpose of this case study is to describe the actual and potential impact of information technology on professional firms. The professional commenting here highlights key issues for practice leaders to consider when installing, developing and managing information systems.

Shane Godbolt is Regional Librarian for North West Thames Regional Library and Information Service which meets the needs of approximately 30 medical and hospital libraries throughout the region. She explains that the move to computerize library systems during the last ten years has required librarians to become expert in the use of computers to organize library information.

Increasingly, librarians are recognized as Information Specialists and consultants for applying Information Technology. They train ordinary people on a daily basis to use highly sophisticated computer systems which allow access to a vast amount of information. Her remarks in this case study are addressed to professionals who recognize the importance of IT but are still considering its implications for their business activities.

Shane says, 'Professionals need to understand the profound affect which the PC [personal computer] has had on every facet of personal and business life. It has had a greater impact than Gutenberg and the printing press because it touches every aspect of life, including the home. With the invention of printing, books didn't get into the home immediately. This took decades. What is happening with technology now is truly revolutionary.'

This change is occurring so quickly because computer users can so easily link up to form *networks*. This allows them to communicate and work together with great efficiency. Shane explains that a network is simply the electronic link created when computers talk to one another. She adds, 'We now have an emerging electronic infrastructure of enormous power. This technology has become so much a part of our environment, that we must *all* take it fully on board. If companies are to survive, they must learn how to manage information. This requires more than taking on isolated [computer] applications of spreadsheets, word processing and database use. We only have to look at our children to see that they are as comfortable with computers as they are referring to books.

'Philosophically, I have to answer some questions for myself about IT applications. Integrating and sharing information is a new concept. Acting on this idea requires redefining traditional boundaries in business between managers, workers, professionals, vendors, customers and clients. We need to think about information flow. It's fine storing information, but how do you get it back? How do you promote flow of information and also make sure that data is integrated so that it can be shared?'

Shane believes that sharing information is essential and that it provides an illustration of the whole being greater than the sum of its individual parts. She explains, 'For example, if we use the appropriate software, we can create documents for storage, be they letters, short reports or notes from a telephone conversation. These go on to a database and are retrievable. When a professional wishes to review a case or visit a client, all of the information about that client is readily available.'

Integrating and managing information through use of databases is at the core of the 'electronic office' and is more efficient and comprehensive than dependence upon banks of filing cabinets containing paper files. In a legal office, for example, there are people performing different functions. Copies of paper documents are often limited to the person who produced them. If these are integrated into a database, then professionals have access to all of the documents relevant to the understanding of a client's affairs.

'It is also far more cost-effective because duplication can be avoided and access is available to a wide range of information sources for research. Consider, for example, telephone directories. I recently received a memo about limiting the use of Directory Enquiries because of the cost per call. Now, as an alternative to this source of information, an organization such as this needs an entire collection of telephone directories. Each directory must be purchased, stored and updated regularly. As well, there is the cost of the time it takes to go to a central location to look for a telephone number. All of this costs far more than calling Directory Enquiries where they have a CD ROM which stores global information.

'Another obvious example is the electronic office. It is more efficient and practical when setting up a meeting to refer to electronic diaries. Instead of secretaries phoning around, schedules can be checked through the computer. And then there is E-Mail which releases us entirely from the constraints of paper and the telephone. Messages are sent E-Mail from PC to PC and are picked up instantaneously.' Even so, Shane proposes that, 'Someone who is wedded to a pen and pad should not feel that this is taken away. What is essential is to recognize that junior people expect to make use of more efficient ways of working.' For the current generation of junior professionals, 'new' technology is just normal practice.

In reference to confidentiality, Shane says, 'We may decide that a confidential letter should not be common office property [if it is stored on a database]. In that case, security levels can be built into the system so that there is *closed access* for some documents and their presence on the system could be kept entirely confidential. It wouldn't even be possible to see that they exist. The technology is so powerful that we can create an integrated system with complete security and safeguards for confidentiality.'

Shane describes the role of the information manager as a vitally important one and that firms should consider either training existing staff or recruiting for this position. This specialist is responsible for purchasing software (computer programs) and hardware (equipment) as well as for the ongoing development and maintenance of the databases. If major purchases are necessary, this manager either provides advice or hires an outside technician or information network consultant. The latter specialist is an expert in creating links between individual computers within an office to form a 'local network' and between networks to form regional and even global links all by way of the computer.

Shane says, 'Information is now a vital resource and must be monitored as closely as finance. So much money is wasted putting in the wrong systems. People should be aware that they need professional advice. Even a very small firm wishing to create a database should contract someone with library information skills, at least on a part-time basis. This would be a person able to work with both the technology and the computer users.

'The development of an IT system requires strategic planning. There has to be a bridge between the computer user and the technical aspects. A successful information system *cooperates* with the way the firm's human population works. What the firm is doing and wishes to do should determine its equipment and software needs. Purchases must *follow* decisions about the firm's information needs. The information manager must be able to work with people so that their needs are served by the technology they purchase.'

Although librarians are not generally perceived in this way, they are on the cutting edge of the IT field: working hand in hand with technology designers and computer vendors and inventing new ways for managing data. In fact, it seems appropriate that librarians should assume the role of information specialists given their traditional function as custodians of society's knowledge base.

In summation Shane says, 'We have to become more flexible and more cooperative in our attitudes towards information. As a professional librarian, I see the value of sharing information because, without this, I cannot provide an effective service. What we must remember is that, at the end of all of our work, there is a patient or a client who needs our help. If we can focus on this, then it becomes easier to harness every available resource to serve that goal.'

THE POLITICS OF INFORMATION

Chapter 3 proposes that information is one of four sources of power within organizations (see page 51). This was true before the electronic revolution which Shane Godbolt describes and the idea has even greater significance now. Particularly where organizations contain strong individual divisions or departments, rivalry is often expressed through information: its access and the way in which each division presents it. The choice to give, receive and withhold information provides a source of considerable power to those who know how to use it.

This is illustrated by the example of a merger of two large teaching hospitals which were renamed and relocated to new buildings. Three years later, there still existed two clearly identified factions working together under one hospital roof. Both continued to find highly creative ways to refuse the use of a single report format, avoid development of a shared database, withhold information crucial to everyday operations and budgeting and generally resist the sharing of information of any kind.

This was certainly an irrational and counter-productive reaction to change. Even so, from the perspective of the medical professionals, the management and clerical staff involved, it was a positive response to maintaining the stability, reliable care, medical approach and historical tradition which they brought with them from two very different hospitals. In the laboratories, teaching theatres, wards and offices, staff in general showed goodwill towards each other and a mutual commitment to the care of patients. Even so, their divided approach ultimately did have an impact on efficiency and, therefore, a negative effect on patients.

Each group would argue, that is if they were absolutely forced to admit that a problem existed, that their approach was the better one and that the other group merely needed to recognize its advantages. Neither group even acknowledged the existence of the hospital's newly developed but virtually unused information system.

In this example, the strategists who initiated the merger shot themselves in the foot long before the new hospital's opening day. The person whom they hired to ensure integration of the purpose-designed information system was only part-time and commuted 200 miles to the new hospital. This choice was based on tight finances and also the belief that most of the work could be done over the phone. They also hired a new hospital chief executive who knew nothing about information management. Although she was willing to learn, she was stuck with a part-time computer consultant on an extended contract who was never there when the system broke down.

Not one of the medical or administrative personnel from either of the two original hospitals had been asked what they needed when the hospital's information system was designed. Instead, they received complicated instructions seemingly written in a foreign language. Although the new system promised enhanced patient care, it was never fully tested. Medical staff laughed at the idea of relying upon it for storage of vital patient data and would not even consider using the system for monitoring patient treatment of any kind.

However aggravating hospital staff would appear to the merger strategists, they were employing creative means to avoid dependency on an information system which none of them trusted. Although this was never discussed openly, they adopted a course of action which they believed to be safer for their patients. This required the two groups to function as subdivisions using two information systems which they already knew how to operate. Gradually, their having separate systems became normal routine and the exercise of their information power was the way in which they provided reliable care for their patients.

TECHNOLOGY RELUCTANCE

Whenever there is resistance to computer technology, there is always a deeper issue to be addressed. In comparison to age-old issues of office politics, the most complex computer technology is far more easily managed. In professional firms, it is still common to have at least one partner refuse to use a computer. There are even professionals in their forties who risibly argue that they are too old to learn new technology. They are not, on the other hand, too old in some cases to take up hang gliding, learn new tax law, study for an advanced degree in soil mechanics or engage in other challenging pursuits. When professionally expert individuals resist an innovation as significant, radical and far-reaching as computer technology, they are saying more to their partners than, 'It's too difficult for me'. Their reluctance signals other messages and their partners benefit the firm by discovering what these are. Among the many options are the following. They could:

- resist taking responsibility for access, analysis and use of massive sources of information
- refuse perceived increases in workload
- fear the loss of status associated with use of a keyboard
- lack an awareness of the benefits and absolute necessity of computer use.

Whatever the source of their resistance, there is only one way to discover the truth. Partners serve their firm and their colleagues by insisting on a discussion of this matter. New technology is not going away; it is an essential feature of working life and increasingly affects both the content of decisions and the way in which these decisions are made. No one is immune and refusal to participate or develop use of new technology is detrimental to the firm.

NETWORKS

In 1992, the acronym 'LAN' gained common usage among computer enthusiasts. It stands for 'local area network' and refers to the connection of separate computers within a small geographical area, such as an office or a building. The network is formed by linking together separate personal computers by using a device appropriately called a 'bridge'. This allows several computers to share access to memory, printers and data storage facilities and results in a single system of considerable power.

It is also possible to link formerly incompatible pieces of equipment. 'Big box' machines, such as mainframe computers, and 'small box' equipment, such as desktop terminals, Unix workstations or Macintosh models can now be organized so that they work together. One obvious benefit is the potential elimination of 'obsolete' equipment. Machines which formerly could not 'do business together' can now fully cooperate as long as they are compatible with the LAN system requirements.

The development of networks emerged with the creation of a 'client to server' software application. In simple terms, a single computer is designated 'the server' and its task is to coordinate all of the electronic activity of the other 'client' computers linked within the network. The server receives, distributes, borrows and lends information from all of the participating clients whose users (the practice members) continue to generate new data in the form of spreadsheets, letters, reports and so forth.

The server can be a mainframe, a minicomputer or a desktop as long as this machine is powerful enough to handle this demanding role. The clients can be any serviceable computer terminal linked to the network by a bridge. When the networks are connected, then information rapidly circulates from client to server to client so that messages, diary dates, documents and a myriad of other information are readily accessible to any network user.

Even as this chapter is being written, new network developments are emerging. For example, one new software application eliminates the need for a designated server which, not surprisingly, is the most expensive part of a LAN system to purchase, run and maintain. Instead of 'client to server', there are software programs which now allow each client-member of the network to communicate directly with each other client. This is called 'peer to peer' communication. As well, manufacturers of computer equipment, the 'hardware', are producing 'super servers'. These are enhanced personal computers designed specifically to run a network system.

There are also radical developments in WAN, or 'wide area networks'. A WAN refers to the link-up of computer systems across a large geographical area, such as between countries or cities. This link can exist between an individual desktop computer and a commercial database, or between several LANs. Whenever data is transmitted over a great distance, a WAN is in operation.

In the past, WAN link-ups have been routed across expensive kilostream or megastream lines leased from the telecommunications industry. New developments now allow the transmission of data by way of radio waves. This potentially eliminates the need for cables which physically link pieces of equipment together. The technology for this is an electronic card plugged into the back of a computer. This allows the terminal to function rather like a mobile phone.

Radio wave links have applications for LAN as well as WAN because elimination of cables allows greater flexibility for office design. The placement of workstations need no longer be dictated by the presence of a false wall or floor for routing network cables. A temporary need for privacy or the choice to work in clusters become immediately satisfied options because equipment is moveable without need for cable connections.

All of this is relevant to professional firms. Once partners acknowledge that there is an information revolution occurring, their next choice is the extent of their participation. Networks are not necessarily an immediate need for everyone, particularly if a firm has recently upgraded their standalone personal computers so that each has a large memory capacity already. The initial investment in network equipment can be high in terms of cables, bridges, software for 'client to server' usage or for 'peer to peer' and purchase of a server terminal, if necessary. The decision to develop a network should be based on a thorough analysis of the firm's information management needs which, in turn, is based on the partners' long-term vision for the practice (see page 82).

Analysis 13

Part 1

Partners benefit from discussing the following issues.

1   Is the present computer system effective?

2   Are there efficiency advantages to a link-up of all of the firms'
     computer equipment now (electronic mail, shared use of practice
     databanks, project team collaboration and so on)?

3   Are there any disadvantages to this link-up now (costs, disruption
     during transition, time for training and maintaining a LAN, for
     example)?

4   Are the firm's present WAN links used effectively?

Part 2

1   A single partner should assume responsibility for surveying all of
     the support staff and non-partner professionals. They should be
     asked the same four questions in Part 1 with an additional request
     for suggestions. This area is one in which the oldest and most
     senior practice members can expect to learn a great deal from the
     youngest and most junior.

2   Partners discuss their staff's responses to the four questions and
     their suggestions.

The information from this discussion allows the partners to define
where the firm is now in terms of the standard of its equipment and the
sophistication of its usage. This process begins to reveal any dissatisfaction with efficiency and provides the basis for partners to consider how
they would like information technology to be developed within their
firm. A review of the practice mission and their goals (see page 86)
leads to an exploration of how new technology serves the firm in
pursuit of all of the other goals?

    When the partners have an answer to this question as well as an
evaluation of their present system, they benefit the firm most if they

seek advice from the best computer consultant they can afford. Shane Godbolt suggests that librarians or professionals with information management training are appropriate choices. Consultants who are not in any way associated with equipment or software sales are also appropriate. Although sales representatives *potentially* provide unbiased information, historically, they do not.

An outside adviser with specialized knowledge aids the development of a first-rate system which matches the firm's potential for growth. Although a system can be designed in-house by enthusiastic non-specialists, a specialist can objectively address issues of data management, security and expansion so that the firm saves much unnecessary expense in the long run.

LIABILITY

The memory reserves made available through a network open enormous possibilities for a firm. Formerly, when powerful desktop machines stood idle or were used at a fraction of their capacity, their memory was inaccessible. As part of a network, however, their available memory can be kept in use. This allows users of the network to search increasingly extensive databanks in-house and also draw upon memory-demanding link-ups to a WAN. The firm's clients benefit considerably from this service because it leads to thoroughly researched advice.

The issue of research liability is now under debate. At the heart of the discussion is the reliability of traditional manual research methods. The question: Where these methods are used exclusively, can a firm now be considered negligent if vital, precedent-setting information could be made available to the firm through a computer search of commercial databanks? This issue is far from resolved and it is one which partners benefit from considering when planning data analysis capability and investing in information management technology.

Because industry is ahead of the professions in computer applications, professional firms actually have a distinct advantage. Partners are now in a position to learn from the computer system errors made in manufacturing and government during the last 20 years with particular focus on network experiments since 1992. Although many practices are currently computerized, they are now reaching a new stage of growth. Before partners make major new investments in a network system, they can study the best and the worst of past industrial solutions.

THE NEED FOR POLICY

Having made decisions about the firm's information system, the partners' next task is to determine policy for its use. There are certain key areas which require thorough discussion and decision making. These include: access to data, use of equipment, ownership of information, confidentiality, back-up routines, security and others. A policy which is appropriate for one firm is not necessarily applicable to another. This section highlights those topics essential for debate. As Shane Godbolt suggests, clear policies about human needs and practice priorities allow an information manager to choose equipment and software that matches the firm's requirements.

Databases

A database is a means of pooling practice knowledge and information. It integrates this so that the data becomes accessible to approved practice members. This synthesis requires rethinking 'ownership' of information. When data is entered into a computer file, the individual who generated it does not know who eventually will need and use it. There is an element of blind generosity in this process, particularly because many professionals keep their client leads and business information to themselves. Although they willingly share the income from work conducted on behalf of the firm, they do not really consider information about this work to belong to the firm. Information is not yet commonly seen as an asset to be shared.

Information technology entirely transforms the way in which a professional firm operates, in terms of efficiency, organization of projects and people and awareness of interdependence. Partners lose considerable autonomy when a firm becomes computerized because their work leaves an electronic trail behind them which colleagues can readily follow. As well, once the decision is made to pool information, the partners make explicit that data is a practice asset owned collectively (see page 140). Some partners are not ready to take this step, and this offers one explanation for partner-level resistance to practice computerization.

When the benefits of electronic data management are fully understood, professionals more readily accept database development as a fact of business life. Among the advantages to the practice of a single, computerized source of data are:

- the ease of manipulating, changing and updating information
- the possibility of creating a consistent presentation format for reports, letters and other documents
- comprehensive background research by meeting database requirements
- rapid analysis of information from multiple sources inside and outside of the firm.

All of these features are labour and time saving so that tasks that require days of professional time are completed in minutes. This has an obvious impact on client billing and, therefore, on the firm's ability to be competitive.

Even so, disadvantages also result from the development of a comprehensive practice database. One of these is the expense of its management. An information specialist, knowledgeable about networks and security is able to command a premium salary. This is based on their having computer programming and electronic expertise as well as human relations skills to aid computer system design. It has been suggested that a firm needs one data administrator for every ten fee-earning professionals although this number is only an estimate and every administrator need not be equally qualified.

The second disadvantage is the degree of use made of the firm's database. This is a management and planning issue. It refers to the partners' ability to coordinate goals for all five business areas (see page 95). For example, the decision to develop a database is best linked to specific goals for how the information is to be used throughout the firm. If one function of the pooled information is practice development, then partners need also to set goals for its active use. If the firm is to gain real benefit from its investment, the practice plan would include goals to develop facilities (the database), train people and promote the firm through its use. A systematic approach by practice leaders avoids costly computer investments which are never used.

Security

This area is vitally important for partners' review because increasingly practice operations depend upon technology. If the system's security is breached, then data can be manipulated, stolen, misused or destroyed. Key issues are: virus proliferation and illegal access. The *SAC* reference, referred to at the beginning of this chapter, cited poor security as a major information management problem. It is also estimated that billions are lost annually through poorly monitored security systems or security failure.

A security breach can come from inside the firm from employees, contractors and former employees or from outside the firm from WAN links, competitors and hackers. Although governments are responding to new security needs created by technological advances with laws protecting computer programs, legal retribution is no compensation for loss of vital data. Firms are best served by closing every security loophole through human monitoring, special equipment and software which discovers intruders, sets off an alarm and traces the culprits. The more a firm depends upon its data, the greater its need for security measures.

Virus Proliferation

This is a growing cause of concern. A 'virus' is a term used to describe a program which is entered into a computer system having been purposely designed to damage its files and memory banks. Viruses can pass from one computer to another through floppy disks, the contents of which then contaminate a computer's hard disk. When terminals are connected in a network, a virus-laden disk which is entered into one terminal can effectively contaminate the whole system. Potentially, it can also be used to attack a WAN through its link-up to a single terminal.

There are sophisticated equipment and software solutions to protect a computer system from viruses. These include security codes, encryption units and infra-red locking devices. There are also simple and inexpensive responses to the problem. For example, floppy disk vendors provide their product in a variety of colours. Information managers can use colour coding as a security measure so that certain colours are assigned to different departments. In this way, the presence of a 'foreign' disk is detected immediately.

Illegal access

Breaking into a computer system, or 'hacking' as it is also called, is most frequently motivated by three reasons. These are:

- nuisance and data sabotage: to undermine the firm
- fraudulent use of information: to misrepresent or gain materially
- theft: to apply information to a non-firm purpose.

Many computer terminals now come with case locks and built-in pass word protection and yet there should be a practice policy which states clearly what constitutes illegal access and misuse of information. Although correct and appropriate usage may seem the subject of common sense, the complexities of information ownership lead to contradictory definitions of: 'fun', 'just a joke', 'harmless to try', 'didn't know it was private', 'how could that be illegal' and so forth. At least some misunderstandings can be avoided when partners make a clear statement about use of their electronic equipment and the ownership of the firm's data. This avoids having to accuse a mildly curious employee of breaking data protection laws.

Copyright

Partners are liable for any abuse of software copyright by their employees. This area is very important for policy making because copying computer programs can seem completely harmless to staff. The big software companies take a different view and are entitled to take legal action if any infringement is detected.

There is an even more complex issue surrounding copyright. This addresses ownership of documents, letters, reports and so forth. For example, the writer of a letter owns its copyright. If the letter's contents are entered into a computer file, then technically the writer's permission should be sought. As electronic scanning equipment becomes more sophisticated, it is ever more tempting to fill memory banks with other people's written property.

The 'Who will know?' school of management is able to shrug this one off and yet it represents an ethical dilemma for others. Such problems did not exist just a few years ago and now they require immediate attention. People at work are making decisions every day about data protection and this has a subtle influence on society's attitudes about ownership and copyright. Although it is tempting to wait and see how the appropriate international agency interprets copyright law, professionals have an opportunity to contribute to these new developments and shape the future of information management.

PROBLEM – ANALYSIS – DISCUSSION

Problem

A group of six former oil industry scientists decided to form a consultancy firm offering environmental advice to industrial clients. Their commercial and management expertise allowed them to establish a client-base very quickly, and yet this demand for their services required that they launch their activities on a much larger scale than they originally intended. Because they realized that their firm's growth could escalate, they developed a computer network system which could easily be expanded as needed. One of the partners designed this system and organized it so that the memory of each separate computer terminal could be harnessed to form a powerful network of terminals working in cooperation.

Within eight months of the firm's first day of business, the six partners were already celebrating the achievement of all of their first year-end targets. Not only was the firm a financial success, but the partners believed they were providing a valuable service to industrialists who wanted and needed to clean up their environmental act.

Just as the partners were leaving the office together for a celebration dinner, their accountant rushed in to say that a virus was eating all of their billing files. It was uncontrollable as data from file after file arose to the screen and then melted away in strips. The system's designer moved immediately to disconnect the network. He knew that, potentially, the virus could travel to the other terminals and contaminate or destroy all of their memory banks in turn. Unfortunately, he was too late because this was already happening. Horrified, they immediately phoned a computer consultant. Although the systems expert said that she would come right away, she was unwilling to offer any reassurance that their data would be saved. From the partners' description, it certainly sounded to her like a major disaster.

Potentially they faced a complete loss of data: time records for current billing as well as all of their archives, planning documents, lists of business contacts, reports, confidential correspondence, and information from innumerable important files. One of the partners admitted that he had been keeping no paper copies at all because he was experimenting with the idea of a paper-free office. His colleagues were simply too numb to respond.

Just as it seemed impossible for anything to get worse, the office manager came in and asked why they hadn't turned up at the restaurant. When they told her what had happened, she said, 'Good, now maybe you'll pay more attention to security.' Then she added, 'I have never trusted the way this network was set up and so I took it on myself to back the whole thing up every day. Every record is organized on to back-up tapes which are kept in my own safe. Basically, you've only lost work completed during the last hour and our insurance covers equipment damage. Now, if you're ready, let's celebrate the last eight months of success.'

Analysis

1   What was the potential result for the business from this virus
attack?

2   What management issues need further attention in this firm?

3   How can they identify the source of the virus?

4   What would be likely entry points for the virus?

Discussion

Although this problem has a happy ending, an extensive loss of data
has put some firms out of business. The shock of a complete computer
system breakdown can paralyse practice leaders so that they feel unable
to take any action. Traditionally managed firms are likely to maintain
paper back-up and so they are better off than those which depend
entirely on electronic systems and yet are careless about back-up. Even
so, it is extremely difficult to revert to paper management when a
computer emergency requires this.

This firm is very lucky to have an office manager who takes so strong
an interest in the firm's security. Without her intervention, the partners
faced real disaster and yet her back-up was executed covertly. There is
something seriously amiss with a firm's management when security is
not only ignored, but worse, perhaps considered faint-hearted or a
weakness. Macho ideas about risk-taking or 'New Age' idealism about
trusting others are extremes which have no legitimate place in practice
management. A policy for security should be set by practice leaders
rather than left to the discretion of a conscientious manager. These
leaders create strong doubts about the adequacy of their other
computer system policies.

They may be unable to trace the source of the virus through their
own equipment and yet the attack is a criminal offence. The police
could handle the discovery of the culprit by investigating the
accessibility to partners' portable computers. These provide likely
targets for the entry of foreign disks. A virus program could be timed to

destroy data long after it gained entry to the network through the portable computer terminal.

If the partners are in the habit of leaving their equipment unattended when visiting clients or during fieldwork visits, then this is the ideal time for an attack. This behaviour leaves their whole system at risk. Given the controversial nature of the firm's work, there are likely to be many firms and individuals which would benefit from the firm's loss of data.

SUMMARY

This chapter emphasizes the dramatic impact of information technology upon professional firms. It is suggested that practice leaders first determine the firm's information management needs before purchasing equipment or designing a system. This is as much a political and human issue as it is a technical one. The process of establishing a network is described and relevant computer jargon terms are defined. Potential liability arising from failure to use new technology is discussed and essential issues in need of practice policy are highlighted. These include database development, system security and copyright.

Appendix I

Addresses

Chapter references

British Standards Institution
Post Office Box 375
Milton Keynes MK14 6LL
U.K.

HMSO
Post Office Box 276
London SW8 5DT
U.K.

The *SAC* Report
The Institute of Internal Auditors (UK)
13 Abbeville Mews
88 Clapham Park Road
London SW4 7BX
U.K.

Case studies

Mrs Christine Freshwater
Chantrey Vellacott Chartered Accountants
Russell Square House
10–12 Russell Square
London WC1B 5LF
U.K.

Mrs Shane Godbolt
British Postgraduate Medical Federation
North West Thames Regional Library and Information Service
33 Millman Street
London WC1N 3EJ
U.K.

Mr Peter Haigh-Lumby
Gerald Eve Chartered Surveyors
7 Vere Street
London W1M 0JB
U.K.

Mr Richard Kline
Kenneth Leventhal & Company
2049 Century Park East
Suite 1700
Los Angeles, CA 90067
U.S.A.

Miss Mei Sim Lai
Pridie Brewster Chartered Accountants
Carolyn House
29–31 Greville Street
London EC1N 8RB
U.K.

Professor Nina Matheson
Johns Hopkins University
William H. Welch Medical Library
School of Medicine
1900 East Monument Street
Baltimore, MD 21205
U.S.A.

Mr Don Pinchbeck
Innoverve Limited
Laurel House
Woodhall Lane
Hemel Hempstead
Hertfordshire HP2 5PT
U.K.

Mr Michael Pleasants
Innoverve Limited
Laurel House
Woodhall Lane
Hemel Hempstead
Hertfordshire HP2 5PT
U.K.

Mr John Roberts
Chantrey Vellacott Chartered Accountants
Russell Square House
10–12 Russell Square
London WC1B 5LF
U.K.

Consultants

Professor George Brown
George and Judith Brown and Associates
2141 Ridge Lane
Santa Barbara, CA 93103
U.S.A.

Dr Carol A. O'Connor
Vision in Practice Limited
23 Belsize Park Gardens
London NW3 4JH
U.K.

Dr Aubrey Wilson
Aubrey Wilson Associates
6 Lombardy Place
London W2 4AU
U.K.

Appendix II
Legislative References

There are three Acts of Parliament which are relevant to professional firms in the UK. These are:

- The Partnership Act of 1890
- The Limited Partnership Act of 1907
- The Registration of Business Names Act of 1916.

Although these specific Acts do not apply to an international audience, their inclusion here highlights the probable existence of corresponding governmental regulations in other countries. Because a *professional partnership* is a legal entity, each country has legislation which governs its activities.

The *Registration of Business Names* is another issue which typically carries legislation. This refers to firms which operate under a name other than that of its prinicipals. Legal advice should be sought regarding the need to register the use of a business name. In the UK the provisions of this Act do not necessarily apply to firms which continue offering professional services in succession to the principals who originally gave their names to the firm.

Copies of the Acts of Parliament referred to here are available through Her Majesty's Stationers Office (HMSO) with reference to the following numbers:

- 1890: HMSO 010 850 233 3
- 1907: HMSO 010 850 395 X
- 1916: HMSO 010 850 415 8

The address for contacting the HMSO is:

HMSO
Post Office Box 276
London SW8 5DT
Telephone: (071) 873-9090

Bibliography

Allsopp, Michael, *Management in the Professions: Guidelines to improved professional performance*, Business Books, London, 1979.

Argenti, John, *Practical Corporate Planning*, Unwin Hyman, London, 1989.

Argenti, John, *Predicting Corporate Failure*, Institute of Chartered Accountants in England and Wales, London, 1984.

Bateson, Gregory, *Mind and Nature: A necessary unity*, Bantam Books, New York, 1980.

Bazerman, Max H., *Judgement in Managerial Decision-making*, Wiley, New York, 1986.

Bennis, Warren, *On Becoming a Leader*, Addison-Wesley, Reading, MA, 1989.

Bennis, Warren, and Nanus, Burt, *Leaders: The strategies for taking charge*, Harper & Row, New York, 1985.

Bronson, Denise E., Pelz, Donald C., and Trzcinski, Eileen, *Computerizing Your Agency's Information System*, Sage, Beverly Hills, CA, 1988.

Burns, James MacGregor, *Leadership*, Harper & Row, New York, 1978.

Carr-Saunders, A. M., and Wilson, P. A., *The Professions*, Associated Business Press, London, 1980.

Cook, Mark, 'Experiments on Orientation and Proximics', *Human Relations, 23*, 1, 61–76.

Cooper, Terry L., *The Responsible Administrator: An approach to ethics for the administrative role*, Kennikat Press, London, 1982.

Dainow, Sheila, and Bailey, Caroline, *Developing Skills with People*, Wiley, New York, 1988.

Davenport, Thomas H., Eccles, Robert G., and Prusak, Laurence, 'Information Politics', *Sloan Management Review*, Fall, 53–65, 1992.

Edelman, Murray, *The Symbolic Uses of Politics*, University of Chicago Press, Chicago, 1967.

Finkler, Steven A., *The Complete Guide to Finance and Accounting for Nonfinancial Managers*, Prentice-Hall, Englewood Cliffs, NJ, 1983.

Fisher, B. Aubrey, *Perspectives on Human Communication*, Macmillan, New York, 1978.

Galbraith, Jay R., *Organization Structure*, Addison-Wesley, Reading, MA, 1977.

Getz, Lowell, and Stasiowski, Frank, *Financial Management for the Design Professional: A handbook for architects, engineers and interior designers*, Whitney Library of Design, New York, 1984.

Gibbs, John, *A Practical Approach to Financial Management*, Financial Training Publications, London, 1980.

Grant, Peter, *Management and Financial Control in the Professional Office*, Business Books, London, 1971.

Guy, Mary, E., *Professionals in Organizations*, Praeger, New York, 1985.

Handy, Charles, *Understanding Organizations*, Penguin Books, London, 1985.

Hargie, Owen, ed., *A Handbook of Communication Skills*, Routledge, London, 1986.

Hay, Susan, *Are You Negligent?: A guide to professional liability and indemnity options*, Economist Publications Ltd., London, 1987.

Hersey, Paul, and Blanchard, Kenneth H., *Management of Organizational Behaviour: Utilizing human resources*, Prentice-Hall, Englewood Cliffs, NJ, 1977.

Janger, Allen R., *Matrix Organization of Complex Businesses*, Elsevier, Amsterdam, 1983.

Kingdon, Donald R., *Matrix Organization*, Tavistock, London, 1973.

Knight, Kenneth, ed., *Matrix Management: A cross-functional approach to organization*, Gower, London, 1977.

Lerner, Michael, *Surplus Powerlessness*, Institute of Labor and Mental Health, Oakland, CA, 1986.

Lewin, Kurt, Lippitt, Ronald, and White, Ralph, 'Patterns of Aggressive Behaviour in Experimentally Created Social Climates', *Journal of Social Psychology*, *10*, 271–99, 1939.

Lewin, Kurt, 'Psychology of Success and Failure', *Occupations*, *14*, 9, 926–930, 1936.

Madsen, Vagn, and Polesie, Thomas, *Human Factors in Budgeting: Judgement and evaluation*, Pitman, London, 1981.

March, James G., *Decisions and Organizations*, Basil Blackwell, New York, 1988.

May, Judith V., *Professionals and Clients: A constitutional struggle*, Sage, London, 1976.

Merry, Uri, and Brown, George I., *Neurotic Behavior of Organizations*, Gardner, Cleveland, OH, 1986.

Moore, James F., 'Predators and Prey: A new ecology of competition', *Harvard Business Review*, *71*, 3, 75–86, 1993.

O'Connor, Carol A., *The Handbook for Organizational Change*, McGraw-Hill, London, 1993.

The Oxford English Dictionary (2nd edition), Vol. I. Clarindon Press, Oxford,1989.

Russo, J. Edward, and Schoemaker, Paul J. H., *Confident Decision-making* Piatkus, London, 1991.

Systems Auditability and Control, Institute of Internal Auditors (UK), London, 1992.

Scott, Bill, *Communication for Professional Engineers*, Thomas Telford, London, 1984.

Shapero, Albert, *Managing Professional People: Understanding creative performance*, The Free Press, New York, 1985.

Shycon, Harvey K., 'Measuring the Payoff from Improved Customer Service', *Prism*, *1*, 71–81, 1991, Arthur D. Little, Cambridge, MA.

Smith, Kenwyn, 'Philosophical Problems in Thinking about Organizational Change', in P. S. Goodman, ed., *Change in Organizations*, Jossey-Bass, San Francisco, 1982.

Smith, Kenwyn, and Berg, David, *Paradoxes of Group Life*, Jossey-Bass, San Francisco, 1987.

Sveiby, Karl Erik, and Lloyd, Tom, *Managing Knowhow*, Bloomsbury, London, 1987.

Torstendahl, Rolf, and Burrage, Michael, eds., *The Formation of Professions: Knowledge, state and strategy*, Sage, London, 1990.

Visart, Nicole, 'Communication Between and Within Research Units',

In Frank M. Andrews, ed., *Scientific Productivity: The effectiveness of research groups in six countries*, Cambridge University Press, Cambridge, 1979.

Webber, Alan M., 'What's So New About the New Economy?', *Harvard Business Review*, *71*, 1, 24–42, 1993.

Wilson, Aubrey, *Practice Development for Professional Firms*, McGraw-Hill, London, 1984.

Wilson, Aubrey, *The Marketing of Professional Services*, McGraw-Hill, London, 1972.

White, Ralph, and Lippitt, Ronald, *Autocracy and Democracy: An experimental inquiry*, Harper & Brothers, NY, 1960.

Index